Marriage Needs Maintenance

By

Ron and Diane Geyer

Marriage Needs Maintenance

Published by:
Intermedia Publishing Group, Inc.
P.O. Box 2825
Peoria, Arizona 85380
www.intermedia pub.com

ISBN 978-1-935906-01-8

Copyright © 2010 by Ron and Diane Geyer
Printed in the United States of America

No part of this publication may be reproduced, stored in a retrieval system, or transmitted in any form by any means – electronic, mechanical, digital photocopy, recording, or any other without the prior permission of the author.

All rights reserved solely by the author. The author guarantees all contents are original and do not infringe upon the legal rights of any other person or work. No part of this book may be reproduced in any form without the permission of the author.

Cover Art Courtesy of Joey Quinones at Tech-xperts.com

Table of Contents

Acknowledgements	i
How and Why this Book will Work for You & Your Marriage	iv
Introduction	vii

PART ONE

Chapter 1	-	Marriage is ONEderful	3

PART TWO

Chapter 2	-	H	=	Head	11
Chapter 3	-	U	=	Understand	39
Chapter 4	-	S	=	Show	49
Chapter 5	-	B	=	Bible	79
Chapter 6	-	A	=	Agreement	89
Chapter 7	-	N	=	Nurture	99
Chapter 8	-	D	=	Diligent	107

PART THREE

Chapter 9	-	The Role of the Wife	117
Chapter 10	-	The Role of Respect	123
Chapter 11	-	A Godly Wife is Wise	127
Chapter 12	-	How Wives Influence their Husbands	135
Chapter 13	-	How Wives Inspire their Husbands	141
Chapter 14	-	W = Worker	149
Chapter 15	-	I = Instructor	161
Chapter 16	-	F = Friend	167
Chapter 17	-	E = Example	177

Chapter 18	-	Be the Woman/Wife God Has Called You To Be	183
Chapter 19	-	Protecting Your Husband	193

PART FOUR

Chapter 20	-	Help Is Here	205

Acknowledgments

To GOD be the glory for the things He has done. Oh that I could sing! What a joyful melody I could make, but I can't, so I won't. Instead, I will take this opportunity to say that Ron and I will be forever grateful and thankful to **HIM** for taking a couple of drug addicted hippies, and making something **ONE**derful.

Who would of thought about taking two very stoned people, crawling around the room on their hands and knees because it was too hard to get up and walk, and speaking into their heart **"God has something special for us to do."** No one but **GOD** could have dreamed up the life **He** has given us.

Why do we love THEE, let me count the ways.

- **You** caused Ron and I to meet and fall in love, and yes, even to live together for those many years.
- **You** personally visited us one desperate night and spoke dreams into our lives, impossible dreams, yet **YOU** have caused them all to come true.
- **You** drew me to a job where I met Cyndy, who prayed for me as I tried to get her fired. She covered up my drug use on the job so that I wouldn't get fired, until she led Ron and I to the Lord. Words could never express our gratitude to her.
- **You** delivered me instantly from an eighteen-year cigarette habit during that time, even while I cursed the man of God and called him a charlatan.
- **You** performed miracles for us in our finances through our roofing company and grew it into a company of integrity **YOU** could be proud of as

we lifted up the name of Jesus through millions of tracts passed out through the years.

- **You** led us to Lakewood Church, and John & Dodie Osteen, where our foundation in the things of God causes us to stand strong and trust God always. They saw to it that the Five-Fold Ministry was presented as a gift from God to us, and we can still remember each and every gift and the messages they taught.

- **You** caused a new chapter to begin in our lives after Pastor John Osteen went home to be with **You**. As Lakewood Church grew and grew under Pastor Joel, **You** led us to get more and more involved in helping meet the need of our new brothers and sisters that were coming to know the Lord and making Lakewood their home.

- **You** placed us in the path of Dr. Vaughn Bryant, Director over Family Life, who trained us, mentored us and encouraged us to help marriages at Lakewood. He taught us how to read the Bible with a "married view" and showed us how to apply that to marriages, ours and theirs.

- **You** gave us a platform to teach what we were learning. A way to watch **You** give "New Birth" to marriages, strength to struggling ones, and even "Life" to dead ones.

- **You** opened up doors of opportunities for us to share **Your** word and **Your** wisdom to help see marriages become all that **You** designed and desired them to be.

- Now this, **You** stirred up the gift in us, **You** have allowed the passion for marriages to rise and **You** have given us the means to share it with the world by writing this book. Who but **You** could have dreamed such an impossible dream.

- To the thousands of couples who encouraged us, week after week after week, coming to class when they could have been doing any number of other things. They came with a hunger to see their marriages delivered and restored, and made into something **ONEderful.**

- To the thousands of couples who shared their testimonies and allowed us to see the manifested miracles that God was doing in their marriages and letting us know that we had a part to play in that outcome.

- To the thousands of couples who told us, "You gotta write a book, you gotta get this information out there to the people."

THANK YOU, THANK YOU, THANK YOU!!!!!!!!!!!

To God be the glory for the things He has done.

HOW & WHY this Book will Work for You & Your Marriage

When Ron and I became "born again Christians" and we first started to hear teaching as to what the Bible said, it was emphasized to us over and over again to "not take their word for something but to look up the Scriptures for yourself." Though there was great joy at the unveiling of God's Word as written in the Bible, there was also some sorrow that went along with it as we wondered why we had never been taught that in the "religion" we were raised in. How could such important knowledge be left out or misconstrued as to fit into a certain church's doctrine? We determined that we would always look up for ourselves what was being taught so that we could examine closely what the TRUTH was concerning everything God had to say to us.

Connect the Dots

In a child's activity book, you have an activity called, "Connect the Dots." With pencil in hand, you follow the dots attached to letters starting with A. It will then reveal a previously hidden picture for you to see.

That is what this book will do for you and your marriage. It will connect the dots of Scripture throughout the Bible to reveal a picture God's Word wants to unveil to you for your marriage. It will bring into clarity a TRUTH that was perhaps previously hidden to you into all its fullness and glory.

We will do this by laying out the Scriptures before you in a *line upon line, precept upon precept, here a little there a little,* the **Isaiah 28:9-10 KJV** way, and by using as many different translations of the Bible as we can. The King James

Version, **KJV,** may be the most recognizable to you because it has been used for so long by so many. But the New King James Version, **NKJV,** may be easier to understand as the *thee's* and the *thou's* are removed.

The Living Bible, **LB,** and the New Living Testament, **NLT,** may speak to you more on a level that you can most easily understand since it is written in modern day language. The Amplified Bible, **AMP,** will take you into a deeper understanding of Scripture to uncover further the meaning of what God's Word is trying to say. Then there is the Message Bible, **MSG.** It is so blunt and to the point that it is like a brick, hitting you in the head followed by "DUH !!!!!!!!!!!!" It cuts to the chase and does not beat around the bush; its meaning is clear and unmistakable.

That is why we make no apologies for the number of Scriptures we use, and that is WHY this book will work for You & Your Marriage.

1 Corinthians 2:4-5 KJV *And my speech and my preaching was not with **enticing words of man's wisdom**, but in demonstration of the Spirit and of power: That your faith should not stand in the wisdom of men, but in the power of God.*

This book is not based on what Ron or I think about something, even if it could be good and sound wisdom. We choose rather to "Connect the dots," of Scripture and reveal what God says about you and your marriage. We will seek to help you see that TRUTH for yourselves and allow the Holy Spirit to guide you in how to appropriate it and make it work in your lives. We will explore God's Word together and dig out the treasure that lays buried in it.

Proverbs 2:6 LB *"The Lord gives wisdom, His every word is a **treasure** of knowledge and understanding."*

We will become prospectors in the gold mine of God's Word and we will be rich indeed. Your personal view of your spouse and your marriage will be forever changed, because of the power that is built into God's Word.

Hebrews 4:12 NLT *For the word of God is **alive and powerful**. It is sharper than the sharpest two-edged sword, cutting between soul and spirit, between joint and marrow. It exposes our innermost thoughts and desires.*

You can then expect miracles to happen. There is no miracle working power in our words, but there is in God's Word. You can see your marriage transformed, not necessarily into what you thought it should be, but better yet, into what God has designed and created it to be.

Romans 12:2 NKJV *And do not be conformed to this world, but **be transformed by the renewing of your mind**, that you may prove what is that good and acceptable and perfect will of God.*

That is why we are excited that you have purchased this book. If you will be obedient to *be a doer of God's word and not a hearer only* **(James 1:22 KJV)** we promise you that there is a miracle for your marriage.

Introduction

Marriage does not do autopilot. Marriage needs maintenance. Your marriage needs maintenance; my marriage needs maintenance... all marriages need maintenance. This book will begin to provide you with the necessary maintenance that is needed to help you achieve your God ordained purpose in a marriage, which is, becoming ONE with your spouse.

Marriage needs maintenance; there is no question about it. We maintain our homes and yards, our vehicles, our financial portfolios, our teeth, our health, our children... the list is endless. But who of us can say today that we are applying the same effort and dedication to maintaining the most important gift we have from God... our marriage. We put our marriages on auto pilot and expect them to run smoothly with little or no effort involved. We plan on addressing marital issues at a later date and only when trouble arises do we begin to respond. Unfortunately, over 60 percent of the time it's too late and we wind up paying the penalty for this passiveness in separation and divorce.

This book will help you understand what your marriage is as defined by the creator of marriage... God. In addition to helping you understand marriage, this book will also paint for you a practical, biblical picture of how that marriage should look. As we tell those in our classes at Lakewood, we don't fix broken marriages, we build healthy ones. In the process of building that healthy marriage, you should be able to discover what needs fixing and how to fix it. You may have to rip out the bad plumbing, you may have cracks in the foundation, you may need a new roof on your marriage, and those are things that will be revealed to you in the light of God's Word. Then, we will help you install whichever home repair is needed, as we help you construct that new marriage.

The complete Marriage Needs Maintenance Program is over twenty weeks and includes teaching on Husbands and Wives' Roles, Personalities, Love Languages, Foundational Power Pillars, Communication, Conflict Resolution and Intimacy on five Levels. We will go into what the Bible teaches on these in future books. But for now, in this first book in the series, we will begin with Husband and Wife Roles. Marriage begins with God and God begins with the man and so too shall we as we bring new light into the heart of husbands and wives.

God has placed a tremendous calling on husbands. He calls the man to a task, that of showing love to his family. The same love Christ shows to the church. He calls the wife to a man. God has placed tremendous power in both, to be able to fulfill this purpose within the marriage. As men, we need to understand ourselves, we need to understand our assignment and we especially need to understand our wives. In today's society, passivity won't work. The leadership void that has been created yet remains, but through this book and the application of its principles, you will be able to grow and see God's greatness in you revealed.

There is power given to wives also from God to help Him mold husbands into what they need to be to serve our wives and our families. Ladies have a unique gifting and relationship with and through the Holy Spirit that will enable them to hear from God and encourage us men in our ability and efforts to obey Him. The power placed in wives to do this is unparalleled in society today. Learn what being married to a man really means. Discover the challenges within that role as God uses wives to reveal His perfect plan of ONEness through their sacrifices.

Truth be told, we men have the greatest ability to reveal who God is to this generation. We have the specific assignment of revealing God in His greatness to our families. Like it or not, know it or not, we have already committed to doing just that. When you open this book, your accountability for your assignment will reach a new level. When you open this book, you will see our God as you have never seen Him before.

It's never too late to get started, to redirect or recommit to becoming the husband or wife of excellence we all thought we would be when we got married. For us men it's time to get back up on that white horse and allow our wives and children to know us as we really are.

Wives, recognize the awesome power available to you through your faithfulness in serving, and discover the ability within you to bring your husband to Christ. Enough is enough. We are God's very best, made in His image and our greatness is revealed in the love we show each other.

Our heart is to see the honor of marriage restored. Yes, it's a large dream with an even bigger task ahead of it, but we serve such an awesome and loving God. We believe with all our hearts the time of visitation from God for husbands and wives in marriage is right here, right now, right for America, and right for the world.

Part One

Chapter 1

Marriage is ONEderful

Marriage does not do auto pilot. Never has, never will. Marriage needs maintenance. Marriage needs daily, intentional efforts by both spouses to invest their very best in each other. The third partner of this marriage union, God Himself, is already investing His best in each of us through Jesus Christ and His Word. Therefore, no less than our best will do. Remember, marriage is a trinity relationship designed by God to help us reveal Him to each other, our families, our friends, our neighbors, our co-workers, and everyone we know.

> The strength of a nation is in its Churches.
> The strength of a Church is in its families.
> The strength of a family is in the union between a man and a woman in Christ.

That is why we can say, your marriage, your Godly marriage, is the most powerful witnessing tool God has placed on the earth today. Husbands and wives becoming ONE, painting the picture of what ONEness with God in a relationship is supposed to look like.

Genesis 2:24 NIV *For this reason a man will leave his father and mother and be united to his wife, and they will become one flesh.*

There is the reason why we get married... to become ONE. Notice, **Genesis 2:24** is not a who or a what or a where or even a when Scripture... it is a WHY Scripture. When you come across a "why" Scripture in the Bible you need to pay special attention to it. You get to move forward three spaces in the board game of life when you digest fully the meaning of these "why" Scriptures. God the Father is going to give us the reason or the explanation as to why we are to do something.

Growing up as a kid, lots of times when I asked Mom or Dad "Why I had to do something," they told me, "You don't need to know why, just do what I told you to do." Here, God our Father is going to take the time and reveal to us His motive behind His desire for us to marry. It's not to procreate, although obviously that will happen and is necessary. It's not to take pleasure physically in each other, although obviously that will take place too. It's not even to avoid being alone, although surely companionship will be provided through this relationship. No, the ultimate goal in marriage, the reason we get married, the why behind marriage is so that we can become ONE.

Yet it is so much more than just becoming ONE. There is another word in that Scripture after ONE. It's the word "flesh." I am not a huge Bible study kind of guy. My wife will sit there with the concordance, she'll have three or four translations open and she will go on these "Bible odysseys" as we like to call them. God didn't make me like that. I love to read the Bible, I mean, I really do love to read the Bible, but I'm not big on word studies or stuff like that. But God clearly spoke to me one day and told me to check out that word "flesh" in the concordance, and I did. It is fascinating to see what God is saying in that Scripture.

The Hebrew word for flesh is *basar*. It is taken from its root which is also *basar* and that is translated in Strong's Concordance as *...being fresh, full, cheerful ...to announce glad news... messenger, preach, publish, show forth (to bear, bring, carry, preach good) to tell good tidings.*

Basically, what God is saying in **Genesis 2:24 NKJV** is that man shall leave his father and mother and be joined to his wife and they shall become ONE glad messenger of good tidings. Now you can understand why we say that your Godly marriage is the most powerful witnessing tool God has on the earth today; a husband and a wife becoming ONE glad messenger of good news.

Truth be told, that word *basar* is used throughout the Bible and the thought behind it is this... if you are flesh... if you are here on this earth legally with an earth suit... you are to become a glad messenger of good tidings. We are all to be preaching the Good News about Jesus. But in the context of a marriage, we not only have the privilege of telling the Good News, but we have the responsibility of showing what it produces, ONEness in a relationship. In marriage, this ONEness exists between the husband and the wife. In the Kingdom of God, it exists between Christ and the Church.

John 17:11 NKJV *Now I am no longer in the world, but these are in the world, and I come to You. Holy Father, keep through Your name those whom You have given Me that they may be one as We are.*

John 17:21 NKJV *that they all may be one, as You, Father, are in Me, and I in You; that they also may be one in Us, that the world may believe that You sent Me.*

Furthermore, we are not only to be one with each other, but marriage is a "Trinity Relationship." You cannot become "One glad messenger of good tidings" without having a relationship with the One you are to be revealing. You, your spouse and God, all becoming one by the power of the Holy Spirit is the answer to Jesus' prayer to His Father in **John 17.**

God in your relationship should be just as real as your spouse. His presence should be so obvious that you look for Him and see Him in every setting. We tell people if you need to set Him a place at the dinner table to remind you of His presence, you go ahead and do it. After all, marriage is:

> **M**aintaining
> **A**
> **R**omantic
> **R**elationship
> **I**n
> **A**
> **G**odly
> **E**nvironment

It's creating that Godly Environment that is going to keep you strong. It's living in that Godly Environment that will insure your success. It's Maintaining that Godly Environment that will insure your ONEness for all to see.

Once again, you are to live out your marriage with the understanding that it is not just for you. Your marriage has been gifted to you by God, the Creator, with the main purpose of using it to paint a picture of what ONEness in a relationship with God is supposed to look like. Remember,

Jesus said this in **John 17:21 NKJV** ...*they all may be one in Us... that the world may believe that You sent Me.*

MARRIAGE MAINTENANCE TRUTH
Your ONEness in marriage is a witness.

Well then, since marriage is an institution created and ordained by God, where does God begin to teach us about marriage? How does God reveal His perfect plan to us for this union called marriage? Simply stated, once we begin to understand God and to know God, we can then understand His union called marriage. Marriage begins with God and in marriage, God begins with the man. So too will we.

TIME TO TALK

Understanding "why" God commands us or allows us to do something is important. **Genesis 2:24** reveals the reason we get married. Can you see how this knowledge might affect your relationship with your spouse? Talk about how and who in your lives might be affected by this new understanding.

With "ONEness" being the goal in marriage, what are some things that might be working against that today in your marriages?

This chapter suggests you set a place for God at the dinner table to remind you and your children of the necessity of living your lives in His presence. What are some other ways we can "practice the presence" of Christ in our daily lives? List some of the things you are currently doing that promote His presence in your home.

At the very beginning of this Chapter there is a keyword which should define our efforts to achieve ONEness with God and our spouses. What is it?

How can we use this attitude of intentionality to insure we are on the right track? Name some areas where being intentional might help us overcome some things that have held us back in the past.

Part Two

Chapter 2

H. U. S. B. A. N. D.

God has placed the husband in the home to be the **Head**. To fulfill this role effectively, he must **Understand** his wife's needs and desires. He is charged with **Showing** his wife and family what God looks like. He does this by reading the **Bible** daily. To maintain harmony and generate power, he seeks his spouse's **Agreement** for all decisions. Through love, he also **Nurtures** his romantic relationship with her. As he becomes **Diligent** in his marital assignments, God can then bless this relationship.

H = *H*ead

It all begins with love. Man's role in marriage is very basic, it is very simple and as a Christian it is very natural… to love our wives. This is not the love that the world portrays but this love was portrayed best by Christ when He offered himself on the cross and died for His love… the church.

Ephesians 5:25 NKJV *Husbands, love your wives, just as Christ also loved the church and gave Himself for her.*

Husband, if there is only one thing that you remember from this whole book, let it be this: You are commanded by God to Love your wife as Christ loved the church.

Ephesians 5:28 NKJV *So husbands ought to love their own wives as their own bodies, he who loves his wife loves himself.*

Ephesians 5:33 NKJV *Nevertheless let each one of you [husbands] in particular so love his own wife as himself.*

The Bible tells us in **John 3:16 NKJV,** *that God so loved the world that He gave…* It doesn't say that God loved the world, it says that He sooooooo loved the world. I purposely stretched out that word because there is an implied hunger in that Scripture, a deep desire and a passion there. There is eagerness and a need embedded in that Scripture. God sooooooo loved. Did you notice husbands, that sooooooo ought your love be for your wives? There is supposed to be a hunger for your wife, a deep desire and a passion for her. Eagerness and need should be evident in your love for her, just as Christ's love is for the Church and God's love is for the world.

That is the starting point for your role as a husband, to love your wife. That is the motivation which will keep you going when the going gets rough. Jesus Christ will be your example in your assignments. He will paint the picture of your many tasks and responsibilities. As Jesus starts off His assignment as the Head of the church, so too will we start off with the husband's assignment as the Head of the home.

Ephesians 5:23 NJKV *For the husband is head of the wife, as also Christ is head of the church; and He is the Savior of the body.*

1 Corinthians 11:3 NKJV *But I want you to know that the head of every man is Christ, the head of woman is man, and the head of Christ is God.*

H = Head

God gives authority to one in the marriage to be in charge, to receive His orders to fulfill His plan for their lives. He has given this authority to the husband. As Christ IS the head of the church, so too IS the husband head of his wife. That Scripture doesn't say he could be or that he should be. If you are a husband and you have a wife, you are her head. If you are a wife and you have a husband, he is your head. There is no such thing as telling God. "I don't think so!!!!!"

Notice it is to fulfill God's plan and not man's. In most marriages, the husband is busy trying to work his plan instead of God's. Man's authority in marriage is not so he can justify meeting all his fleshly desires, but rather, he uses that authority and power to help meet all the needs of his wife and family. God then equips us with a certain anointing, special powers and even places before us specific challenges which allow us to experience Him on a plane not to be experienced by just anyone.

The Scripture about Christ says that, *He is the Savior of the body.* Before Christ ever became head of the church, He had to become her Savior. He did that by giving His life for her. Some of us men have this backward. We believe that we can use our authority; our headship to get our own needs met first. Yet Christ received His authority when He met our need first. Your role is no different guys.

We use our Headship to be GOVERNORS of our home

Philippians 2:6-7 NKJV *Christ, in the form of God, did not consider it robbery to be equal with God, [there's the authority] made Himself of no reputation [there's the humility] taking the form of a bondservant [there's the assignment].*

MARRIAGE MAINTENANCE TRUTH
Leadership Without Humility is Tyranny

We will come to learn as we go through this book that Jesus Christ is always our model for service; He is our ultimate example in everything. Husbands, just like Christ, have been given authority. But, just like Christ, we need to use our authority not to rule and reign, but to sacrifice and serve with humility.

Christ, with all His greatness, with all His perfection, He still had to humble Himself to accomplish His assignment. It is one of the things that make Christ so great… His humility. It is the same thing that will lead you to greatness in your family… humility.

MARRIAGE MAINTENANCE TRUTH
Men, your authority is not so that you can dominate your spouse, it is so you can serve your spouse.

Before we go on, let's look at some Scriptures that describe what a good leader looks like. What are the characteristics of a good leader according to the Word?

Proverbs 16:12 MSG *Good leaders abhor wrongdoing of all kinds; sound leadership has a moral foundation.*

Proverbs 20:28 MSG *Love and truth form a good leader; sound leadership is founded on loving integrity.*

H = Head

We men need to allow God to form us into good leaders in our homes. He does it by creating in us hearts of integrity. A heart of integrity is a heart that loves. In my case, I love Diane. My love towards Diane is perfect, because my heart has been born again, and it has the love of God inside it. I never question my love for Diane, nor do I doubt my love for Diane. My mind may get a little screwy now and then, but my heart is perfect toward her.

Love and Truth form a good leader. God has already given us His love… *the love of God has been poured out in our heart by the Holy Spirit* **(Rom. 5:5 NKJV)**. That's good, but we need another component. We need truth. Truth comes from the Word. Truth and love together form a good leader. Better yet! How about we love that truth? I love Diane, I love truth and God now has the environment in which He can begin to form me into the good leader He needs me to be. The leader my wife and family needs me to be.

This is not hard guys. I choose to step into my God given role as Head of my home. I choose to do those things that He has called me to do. Then it stands to reason that He will equip me with all that I need to accomplish this task. God doesn't tell us to do something and not create in us the ability to do it. He doesn't tell us to do something and not equip us for the task.

Finally, the last ingredient to becoming a good leader is to have a sound moral foundation. Where do you learn right and wrong behavior? It comes from the Word and spending time there with God and in prayer.

2 Timothy 3:16-17 NKJV *All Scripture is given by inspiration of God, and is profitable for doctrine, for reproof, for correction, for instruction in righteousness: that the man of God may be complete, thoroughly equipped for every good work.*

Men, your wife, your children, and your marriage are a good work. It is the good work you chose to do when you got married. Let's look at the specifics of this good work as it applies to marriage.

Ephesians 5:26 NKJV *that He might sanctify and cleanse her with the washing of water by the word.*

As we as husbands love our wives as Christ loves the Church, we can see a picture formed of how to do this. If in the case of Christ loving the Church, that loving act produced sanctification and cleansing, then, we too as husbands have the same responsibility and privilege. When we do that, love our wives as Christ loves the Church, we see that our headship will produce holiness and purity.

Remember, if Jesus is doing it or has done it for the Church, then we are to be following His example and doing it for our wife. If Jesus washes the Church with the Word, then we wash our wife with the Word. If Jesus gives Himself for the Church, even dying for the Church, then we do the same for our wife. If Jesus ever lives to make intercession for the Church, then we ever live to make intercession for our wife.

A good spiritual leader will not only be holy and pure, **1 Peter 1:16 NKJV,** *Be holy; for I am holy,* but he will also be used to help produce holiness and purity in those that follow him. The principle being, if the head be holy and pure, then the body is holy and pure. This is attained *"by sanctifying and cleansing her [your wife] with the washing of water by the word."*

What on earth does that mean? It really doesn't mean anything on earth but it is a spiritual truth that allows husbands the privilege and responsibility of representing God to their wife on a level that no one else on the earth can. Let us look at a Scripture that talks about how God cleanses us.

1 John 1:9 NKJV *If we confess our sins, He is faithful and just to forgive us our sins and to cleanse us from all unrighteousness.*

Since we husbands are to follow the *"love as Christ loved"* pattern that Jesus sets forth for us, then, it is only fitting that we forgive and cleanse as He does.

Ephesians 5:27 NKJV *That He might present it to Himself a glorious church, not having spot, or wrinkle, or any such thing: but that it should be holy and without blemish.*

Another translation uses the word "RADIANT." Webster defines it this way, beaming with light or brightness, kindness and love. If I, as a husband, am suppose to love my wife as Jesus loves the church, then, I should be able to produce the same result in my wife that Jesus produces in the church. That love should produce – RADIANCE.

As a husband, my wife's holiness and purity is my charge, one of my responsibilities. But my reward is a wife who is spotless in her marriage. No wrinkles, no griping, no complaining, no rebellion. Is this possible? If I, as a husband, fulfill my task of HEADSHIP as Jesus fulfilled His task, then yes, it becomes possible with Jesus as my Head.

TIME TO TALK

Christ used His authority not to judge us or order us around, but as a perfect picture of how God expects authority to be used. What parallels can we draw from His service to us and our service as husbands? Talk about areas where your physical dominance is being used for service in your home.

In **Philippians 2** we see the attitude of Christ in His role as a servant revealed. Notice humility is the key for Him being able to do this. Might this be an encouragement for us guys to help us in this area? Can you identify an area or two where pride may have hindered you from using your leadership calling to serve your spouse?

Discuss these two Scriptures in Proverbs about how good leaders are formed and how they act. Discover what God's Spirit says to you. Allow Him to grow you and correct you and place you on the right track as you do this.

Can you see how important a role the Word of God plays in allowing God to form you into a good leader? This would be a great time for you to commit to a renewed effort in your Bible reading. If you were to begin reading the Bible, maybe even for the first time, where would you go for a Bible reading plan? Is there someone who could point you in a direction to get you started? Consider making reading your Bible a priority this week.

We use our Headship to be GUARDIANS in our home

In order to effectively fulfill this aspect of our leadership, we men need to understand that guarding our homes begins by us guarding ourselves!

Malachi 2:14-15 NIV *You ask, "Why?" It is because the Lord is acting as the witness between you and the wife of your youth, because you have broken faith with her, though she is your partner, the wife of your marriage covenant. Has not the Lord made them* *one? In flesh and in spirit they are His. And why one? Because He was seeking godly offspring. So guard yourself in your spirit, and do not break faith with the wife of your youth.*

What a great Scripture and what a great Word from the Lord. God is speaking directly to husbands here. Husbands are to *"guard yourself in your spirit."* Men, you can't give what you don't have. You can't guard your home as you should unless you first *guard yourself.* You need to *guard yourself* before you can stand watch over your wife, your children, your home, your health, and your finances. You have been given the job of being the watchman over any and everything that concerns your family and home.

Before we go any further, we must address certain issues. In the last seven years we have ministered to thousands of couples through one on one mentoring programs and through classroom settings. I would say that the number one problem facing men today without question is sexual impurity.

As shocking as it is, we have seen no difference in the men that call themselves Christians and the men of the world. Infidelity is rampant; pornography is a stronghold in the lives of a large portion of Christian husbands. I believe that sexual immorality is the number one spirit in our nation that seeks out men to destroy them. Until we in the Church get this behind us, we will never be the men of God in our homes that we were meant to be.

I myself grew up with pornography and fell victim to its powers and deceptions until it became a stronghold in my life. Being trapped in this area was one of the things that brought me to Christ. I am fifty-nine years old as I write this and I grew up in the 70s with drugs, alcohol and the sexual promiscuity that went with that lifestyle. I was heavily into drugs... yet I felt I could lick it anytime I chose.

I drank and smoked both cigarettes and pot. I lived off of speed for years and still felt I could quit anytime... but I knew I was held captive by pornography. I was trapped and I knew it. When I came to Christ all the drugs, all the alcohol and all the pornography and the nasty sins that came with it were gone.

You can't tell someone like me there is no God. You can't tell someone like me there is no power in the Cross. You can't tell me Jesus Christ isn't the same today as He was yesterday and how He will be forever.

So, where does that leave you, man of God, husband who is reading this book? What does it mean to you Christian Brother who cries out for deliverance every night; you who curses his weakness and weeps after another failure time and time again? I can tell you this, all your crying and shame, all your anger and broken promises won't help until you learn to hate the sin and come to a saving knowledge of Christ. I am not talking about having a mental acknowledgment of what Jesus has done, but I am speaking about having an encounter with God through Jesus.

Then, you MUST choose to love the Word of God. When I got saved God gave me grace and delivered me. Thank you Jesus! But there was a price to be paid to STAY free and the price was and is my vigilance, and my vigilant action is me reading the Word. When babies are born, they are born with an appetite. You, as a baby Christian, were born with an appetite and that appetite is for the Word of God.

When I was born again, I had a supernatural hunger for the Word. We all get it, it's just that some of us eat and some of us starve. I was so hungry for God. I read that Bible front to back four times in my first year. I loved my freedom! I loved what God was doing for me and to me and now, at long last, through me. But it would not have been possible

H = Head

with me staying trapped in pornography. Sure, God set me free in the new birth, but then it was incumbent upon me to guard myself. And now, it's incumbent upon you men to guard yourselves in the spirit.

I love what Jesus said about Satan. He said in **John 14:30 NKJV**, *I will no longer talk much with you, for the ruler of this world is coming, and he has nothing in Me.*

I can truthfully say that now... Satan has nothing in me. Guys, it's the place of your power. You must get free, stay free and then set free those in your sphere of influence. Satan is under no obligation to listen to you, if you are under his dominion in the area of sexual immorality. This is not optional men. You must get free to be the head of your home that Christ commands you to be. You remain weak and indifferent to spiritual things when you are trapped. You become blind to spiritual truths.

These sins of sex don't stand alone either, they come with friends. You begin lying to cover up your indiscretions. Lying is just about the worse thing you can invest in your marriage. When we as men lie to our spouses we have essentially cut ourselves off from receiving truth.

Galatians 6:7 NKJV *Do not be deceived, God is not mocked; for whatever a man sows, that he will also reap.*

If I am investing lies in my relationship with my wife, that will prevent me from receiving truth from God's Word in my relationship with Him. And guys... you must have Truth. He is the cornerstone of everything your life is built on.

I know I painted a hard picture, but the tale doesn't have to end there, in weakness and defeat. No, the Bible says in

1 Corinthians 15:57 NKJV, *But thanks be to God, who gives us the victory through our Lord Jesus Christ.*

There's the promise. Thank you Jesus... okay, but now how do I get there? Yes, there is work to do. Don't forget, we are talking about husbands providing guardianship in their homes. Let me give you three Scriptures that held and helped me and now hold my freedom to this very day.

NUMBER 1

Proverbs 16:6 KJV *By mercy and truth iniquity is purged: and by the fear of the LORD men depart from evil.*

This is the Word of God. This is your spiritual food, consider this your breakfast. Forget about American Express, don't leave home without this... MERCY. God has given you mercy, *new mercy every morning* **(Lam. 3:22-23 NKJV).** Dear brother, start again, start over, God gives do-overs. Begin today. Drink deeply of His mercy when you wake up and don't leave home without it.

But look, the Scripture says by mercy and truth iniquity is purged. Sexual sin in our lives has become iniquity and we have become held by the cords of our sins. Mercy alone will not purge iniquity. It needs help. No problem guys... God sends help in the form of truth. I just love God's Word! He provides the mercy, free of charge, it's yours, and all you have to do to get it is wake up tomorrow morning. But He leaves you to dig out truth. *Jesus is the truth*, **(John 14:6 NKJV)** but you have to eat it. You have to open the book, get in the Word and learn truth.

Jesus said in **Matthew 11:28-30 LB,** *Then Jesus said, "Come to me, all of you who are weary and carry heavy* *burdens, and I will give you rest. Take my yoke upon you. Let me teach you, because I am humble and gentle at heart, and you will find rest for your souls. For my yoke is easy to bear, and the burden I give you is light."*

Amen! Chew on that Scripture every morning... have it for breakfast. Put the Wheaties box down! Forget about the breakfast of Champions, but instead have breakfast with the Champion.

NUMBER 2

Psalm 119:9 NKJV *How can a young man cleanse his way? By taking heed according to Your word.*

Make this one your daily lunch guys. How do we get and stay sexually clean? By taking heed to the Word.

The Amplified Version... *By taking heed and keeping watch [on himself] according to Your word [conforming his life to it].*

The Message Version... *By carefully reading the map of your Word.*

The New Living Translation cuts to the chase... *By obeying your word.*

NUMBER 3

This last Scripture really holds me accountable in so many ways. But it is absolute dynamite where sexual freedom is concerned.

2 Corinthians 10:4-6 KJV *(For the weapons of our warfare are not carnal, but mighty through God to the pulling down of strongholds ;) Casting down imaginations, and every high thing that exalted itself against the knowledge of God, and bringing into captivity every thought to the obedience of Christ; and having in a readiness to revenge all disobedience, when your obedience is fulfilled.*

Paul is talking about your spiritual weaponry here. Basically, he says that one of your most powerful weapons is going to be the ability to take thoughts captive. Not just thoughts generically speaking, but taking thoughts captive that are contrary to God's Word. He also mentions God's standard for thinking... every thought captive.

That's right. God expects you to take every thought captive. But fret not; it's not in your own strength that you are doing this. I tried bringing thoughts captive to the obedience of Ron... it doesn't work. But look, it says here to the obedience of Christ. If we read further we see we get a second chance at this, *being ready to revenge any disobedience* but only *when your obedience is fulfilled.*

You will need to win the battle for your mind to solidify your freedom men. Notice I said "for" your mind and not "of or in" your mind. Please know this, your mind is in a battle, but the battle is not in your mind. If it was, we would all go around being schizophrenic. No, your mind is to be a weapon in this fight.

Your mind is not the battlefield. It is part of your armor. It is the mind of Christ whereby you take every thought captive. It is a weapon that enables you to pull down strongholds. Look at it this way, in the 1940s, during World War II, America was in a war, but the war was not in America. It's the same way with your mind, your mind is in a battle, but the battle should not be in your mind.

Paul writes in **James 1:8 KJV,** *A double minded man is unstable in all his ways.* Verse 7 says, *"let not that man think he shall receive anything of the Lord."* In **Romans 7:25 NKJV,** *I thank God through Jesus Christ our Lord. So then with the mind I myself, serve the law of God; but with the flesh the law of sin.* We serve God with our minds. We also *renew our mind* according to **Romans 12:2 NKJV.**

In Peter, we see that our minds once again are weapons in our warfare. **First Peter 4:1 NKJV,** *Therefore, since Christ suffered for us in the flesh, arm your selves also with the same mind, for he who has suffered in the flesh has ceased from sin.*

So, once we deal with our sin problem, then we can walk in the fullness of the spirit and become the true guardians of our home that our family desperately needs us to be. The ability to be able to do this is because of what God has placed within us.

1 John 2:20 NKJV *You have an anointing from the Holy One, and you know all things.*

1 John 2:27 NKJV *The anointing which you have received from Him abides in you....*

The Bible says in **1 John 4:17 NKJV** *...as He is, so are we in this world.* Men, that is who you are, right here, right now for your family. Jesus is our example in everything. **John 13:15 NKJV,** *For I [Jesus] have given you an example, that you should do as I have done to you.* Jesus is our example of a GUARDIAN, a Servant, an Intercessor, a Priest and a Shepherd.

Philippians 4:7 NLT *His peace [God's peace] will GUARD your heart and mind as you live in Christ Jesus.* There's the GUARDIAN.

Matthew 20:28 NLT *For even the Son of Man [Jesus], came here not to be served but to SERVE others, and to give my life as a ransom for many.* There's the SERVANT.

Hebrews 7:25 KJV *Wherefore He [Jesus] is able to save them to the uttermost that come unto God by Him, seeing He ever liveth to make INTERCESSION for them.* There's the INTERCESSOR.

Hebrews 2:17 KJV *Wherefore in all things it behooved Him [Jesus] to be made like unto His brethren, that He might be a merciful and faithful high PRIEST in things pertaining to God.* There's the PRIEST.

John 10:11 NKJV *I am the good SHEPHERD: the good shepherd gives his life for the sheep.* There's the SHEPHERD.

Notice these are all tasks that the GUARDIAN is doing. They are not being done "to him" but "by him." As Christ did, we husbands are fully prepared to lay down our lives for our wife and our family in all situations. Remember, we are to *love our wives as Christ loved the Church.* So if this is how Jesus is showing love to the Church, then we take our cue from Him and we show love to our wife in the same manner.

In order to effectively fulfill this aspect of our leadership, we men need to remember that guarding our homes, begins by us guarding ourselves!

1 Peter 5:8 NKJV *Be sober, be vigilant: because your adversary the devil walks about like a roaring lion, seeking whom he may devour.*

Guys, it is you who is in charge. You must be sober, you must be vigilant for the sake of your wife and family. You are to say no and you are to say yes to what spiritual activity goes on in your home.

Matthew 18:18 NKJV *Assuredly, I say to you, whatever you bind on earth will be bound in heaven, and whatever you loose on earth will be loosed in heaven.*

You are the front line of defense for your home. If the enemy chooses to attack my family, he must first come through me. I believe that I AM, ARMED AND READY. I have my defenses up and I give no place to the devil. Therefore, he MAY NOT devour me or my family. He MAY NOT devour our health or our finances, or our business or our relationships, or whatever else is mine to guard.

Ephesians 6:10-11 NKJV *Finally, my brethren, be strong in the Lord and in the power of His might. Put on the whole armor of God that you may be able to stand against the wiles of the devil.*

Men, have you put on the whole armor of God yet? You cannot do a good job of protecting your family if you are not protected yourself. Why?

Ephesians 6:12-13 NKJV *For we do not wrestle against flesh and blood but against principalities, against powers, against the rulers of the darkness of this age, against spiritual hosts of wickedness in the heavenly places. Therefore take up the whole armor of God, that you may be able to withstand in the evil day, and having done all, to stand.*

Men, notice that it is the whole armor of God. Every piece is important and necessary for the warfare that God knows you may be facing. Could you see a soldier tell his commander, "No, No Sir, I don't think that bullet proof vest is necessary." Therefore, you need to know what your armor is and how to use it.

Ephesians 6:14-18 NKJV *Stand therefore, having girded your waist with truth, having put on the breastplate of righteousness, and having shod your feet with the preparation of the gospel of peace; above all, taking the shield of faith with which you will be able to quench all the fiery darts of the wicked one. And take the helmet of salvation, and the sword of the Spirit, which is the word of God; praying always with all prayer and supplication in the Spirit, being watchful to this end with all perseverance and supplication for all the saints.*

Guys, are you faithful about putting your armor on every morning?

That was a trick question. When in a war zone, you never take off your armor of protection or remove your weapons from your person. Our Father knows we have enemies. He knows we will be attacked and He knows where and from whom those attacks will come from. That is why it is vitally important that we keep ourselves protected with the armor of God and keep those weapons He has created for us with us at all times. We are NOT a peace time army. We need these weapons ready twenty-four/seven. Forewarned is for forearmed!

TIME TO TALK

Guarding our homes has got to be one of the most important assignments we have as husbands. What is the starting place for us being able to do this?

The Word is full of references pertaining to men being clean and pure. Which Scripture as mentioned in Guardianship speaks to you about that purity? In what way?

The Bible teaches that we are to *"...take every thought captive."* Do you think that is a realistic expectation? Why... why Not?

If we finish the Scripture above as it is written it says *"...Take every thought captive... to the obedience of Christ."* Does that change your answer?

As you review Guardianship, have your eyes been opened to the ability that God has given you to guard your homes? Discuss one of the items you have learned here about guardianship that you may not have been aware of.

MARRIAGE MAINTENANCE TRUTH
**Passivity is not neutrality in God's Kingdom;
It is surrender!**

We use our Headship to be GUIDES in our home

Psalm 78:72 KJV *So he shepherded them according to the integrity of his heart, and guided them by the skillfulness of his hands.*

Psalm 78:72 NLT *He cared for them with a true heart and led them with skillful hands.*

There's our assignment right there guys concerning your families. You are to GUIDE them with skillful hands. The above Scriptures are written about King David and how he "guided" Israel. Look at the first part of the **KJV** version in the Scripture above. *"He shepherded them according to the integrity of his heart."* I love that phrase, the integrity of his heart. That should cause us to look at ourselves very closely men. Can we say that our hearts are full of integrity concerning our wives? Can I trust my heart to do what is right for my family?

In the movie *Fireproof*, one of the characters challenges the lead actor by telling him "not to follow his heart, but to lead his heart." I chewed on that for a while and while the thought has merit for the unsaved person, once you get Saved and Born Again, your heart is made right with God through the indwelling presence of the Holy Spirit. Now, I trust my heart to do what is right. It's my mind that may get in the way. I choose to allow *the love of God that has been poured out in our hearts by the Holy Spirit* **(Rom. 5:5 NKJV)** to have His way with my decision making process and I will choose what is best for the family over what is best for myself. That is a heart of integrity.

The second part of that Scripture is just as powerful. *"He guided them by the skillfulness of his hands"* or as the Living

H = Head

Bible says, *"he led them with skilled hands."* Once again, we see that David had his hands in the business of shepherding Israel. He had a hands-on approach instead of telling them what to do approach. He got involved with them on many levels. And notice he just didn't lead them with hands; he led them with skillful hands.

Husbands, that implies that King David was very good at what he did. Time for a self-check here men. Are you a skilled husband? Are you taking a "hands on" approach to shepherding and guiding your family? You need to be very good at being a husband. You need to be skilled at it. I believe as revealed in this Scripture, that the way we can become skilled at guiding our families is by having a heart of integrity. That's the key. If we will allow God to create that heart within us, then that is the environment God needs to help us become skilled, "hands on" husbands.

1 Peter 3:1 LB *Wives, fit in with your husbands' plans...*

Notice men, if God has told the wives to fit in with her husbands' plans, then men, we need to have a plan to guide our family.

We need to have a plan to GUIDE our family SPIRITUALLY

Hebrews 10:25 AMP *Not forsaking or neglecting to assemble together as believers.*

Acts 2:42 LB *They joined with the other believers in regular attendance at the apostles' teaching sessions and at the Communion services and prayer meetings.*

The Bible clearly tells us that we are to gather together as Christians. That means going to Church. Part of our headship responsibilities is to take them to church and not just send them to church. The spiritual significance of this is powerful. Our wives and children have seen Dad in charge of the home all week long. Now they need to see him as he recognizes that his power and authority comes from God.

They need to see him acknowledge that there is one greater than he is. That there is someone he is answerable to. They need to see Dad worship God, to see him bring his tithes and offerings in obedience to God. They need to see him placing himself and his family under the teaching authority that is at church. They need to see Dad lift up holy hands as an open sign of surrender to God, and to see that he remembers the covenant Jesus made by partaking in Communion. But that is not all there is to guiding his family spiritually. What about what he does at home?

1 Timothy 2:1-2 NKJV *Therefore I exhort first of all that supplications, prayers, intercessions, and giving of thanks be made for all men, for kings and all who are in authority, that we may lead a quiet and peaceable life in all godliness and reverence.*

1 Peter 2:2 NKJV *as newborn babes, desire the pure milk of the word, that you may grow.*

Husbands need to be praying and they need to be reading their Bibles. If God has told men to be the head of their home and to lead their families, then he has called women and children to follow that lead. Your family is anointed to follow your lead. You want your family to pray, show them by your example. You want your family to read their Bibles, start by reading yours first. We said earlier **1 John 4:17 NKJV** says that *as He is, so are you in this world.* How about allowing that same principle to work for you too? As you are, so too will your family be! Your headship counts for so much more than you may think. It is your greatest tool in raising your children right. It is your foremost ally in gaining the respect that you so desperately crave from your wife. Use your headship to guide your family spiritually, to become all that God wants them to be. Every husband that has been in a marriage has the calling to lead their families. Most husbands are leading them down the road to destruction. We men of God need to make our stand, draw that proverbial line in the sand and say "no more." We must choose to lead them down paths of righteousness, into the presence of the Lord.

M. A. R. R. I. A. G. E.

Maintaining A Romantic Relationship In A Godly Environment. That's on us men!

We need to have a plan to GUIDE our family FINANCIALLY

1 Timothy 5:8 KJV *But if any provide not for his own, and especially for those of his own house, he hath denied the faith, and is worse than an infidel.*

1 Timothy 6:10 KJV *For the love of money is the root of all evil: which while some coveted after, they have erred from the faith, and pierced themselves through with many sorrows.*

Notice, according to the Scripture above, the thing that God has called us to do, provide for our family, has the greatest potential to destroy us – the love of money. Yet, it is the thing that God has called us to pursue at the risk of being called an infidel or an unbeliever if we fail to deliver. We must remember that our job is not our source of provision; it is a means, not the source. God is our source and our way of thanking him for that provision is:

> **Malachi 3:10-11 KJV** *Bring me all the tithes into the storehouse, that there may be meat in mine house, and prove me now herewith, saith the Lord of hosts, If I will not open you the windows of heaven, and pour you out a blessing, that there shall not be room enough to receive it. And I will rebuke the devourer for your sakes.*

Notice that tithing prevents the curse of the love of money from happening. Our former Pastor, John Osteen, used to say that "God doesn't mind you having money, He minds money having you." As GUIDE to my family financially, we bring our tithes to the storehouse and God promises to personally rebuke the devourer for our sake. We need to recognize that money is a tool to be used for the benefit of our family. Our financial plan should include tithing & giving, a budget and savings, and an agreement with our wife on ALL expenditures.

Also, tithing and giving extends to the responsibility of guarding our homes too. By bringing tithes and offerings to the local church we have protected our home from financial calamity. We have secured God's promise that He would personally rebuke the devourer for our benefit.

Notice, we BRING our tithes and offerings. Don't send your tithes and offerings, personally bring them, with your family in tow each time they are due. Let your wives see how this man of God busts his butt at work all week for this money. Then, let the kids watch as Mom and Dad pray over their tithe and present it to the Lord. What a picture of submission to authority you paint for the children when you do this.

This lesson is worth so much more than any teaching you could ever give to your children about finances. The whole family seeing Dad give freely and joyfully to a God they don't see, to a God that maybe they have only heard about, but to a God who Dad thinks enough of, believes in so much that he is willing to work one day out of ten just to honor this God's wishes. After all, God *loves a cheerful giver* **(2 Cor. 9:7 NKJV)**. So much more is caught by our children than is taught them. We as guides in our home have a million chances to teach our kids through our acts of obedience. Men, don't fight against the commands of God, go willingly along with them and look for opportunities to paint pictures for your children through your obedience.

We need to have a plan to GUIDE our family SOCIALLY

It is important to remember that there is more to life than the pursuit of personal accomplishments and business success.

1 Corinthians 10:20 NKJV *Rather, that the things which the Gentiles sacrifice they sacrifice to demons and not to God, and I do not want you to have fellowship with demons.*

2 Corinthians 6:14 KJV *Be not unequally yoked together with unbelievers: for what fellowship hath righteousness with unrighteousness? and what communion hath light with darkness?*

Ephesians 5:11 NKJV *And have no fellowship with the unfruitful works of darkness, but rather expose them.*

Notice as SOCIAL DIRECTOR for your family, the Bible clearly tells you who to stay away from and have no fellowship with. It is incumbent upon you to guide your family in the areas of friendships, especially with your children. They may not have the spiritual maturity in determining who they should be friends with.

As guide, you bring them to church and encourage the kind of relationships you would like them to have. That doesn't mean they have no friendships outside of church, but it means that you control the environment in which they happen. You keep a watchful eye that they are influencing their non-Christian friends rather than their friends influencing them. Fellowship is an important part of a Christian's life, so guide them into right relationships.

1 John 1:3 NKJV *That which we have seen and heard declare we unto you, that you also may have fellowship with us: and truly our fellowship is with the Father, and his Son Jesus Christ.*

Once again guys, since your wife and children are called to follow your lead, let them see you fellowship with God and Jesus through Bible reading, prayer, church attendance, and all the ways that we fellowship with God... they will watch and learn too. You can't go wrong with fellowshipping with the Father and the Son, and the Holy Spirit.

Also, as a husband, you need to be mindful of the social pleasures and needs of your wife.

1 Peter 3:7 NKJV *Husbands, likewise, dwell with them with understanding, giving honor to the wife, as*

H = Head

to the weaker vessel, and as being heirs together of the grace of life, that your prayers may not be hindered.

We must take the lead in encouraging social interaction with our mates. We must continue the dating process in our marriage. We have to know the desires they have and what their needs are on every level. This is especially important if they are a stay at home mom. They need adult fellowship in order to grow.

We husbands are out in the business world, we are on the job, and we are interacting with adults. Our wife is probably home interacting with two-year-olds, children and people who are not as mature as she is. It is on you to make sure we don't create the "wall street dad, sesame street mom" relationship that takes place in many homes today. You can help prevent this by being willing to take care of the kids so she can meet with her friends or encouraging her to take advantage of a Mother's Day Out program at church. You can help by listening to her and talking to her when you get home from work.

Having a social plan for my family doesn't mean we do everything I want to do. No! It is providing what your family needs before your own needs. It is spending time together as a family having fun, enjoying what God has given you. You may need to make time for this. Shut some things down in order for there to be Quality Time spent together.

It is so very important that men take the lead in making their wife feel wanted. We have to come out of our own selves and truly demonstrate the servant nature of Christ. Sure, we are tired after work, we may even be mentally fried, but we still have work to do. Truth be told, it is our most important work that just begins at 5 or 6 or even 7 p.m.

If we allow God to refresh us daily through His Word and His presence, if we will allow Him to work on our "hearts of integrity," if we will let His Word grow us into men with "skillful hands," then we will have the desire and energy to do these assignments as given by God. They will be a joy for us and not a chore and our relationship with our family will be fruitful and glorious!

MARRIAGE MAINTENANCE TRUTH
Intimacy needs to be INTENTIONAL

TIME TO TALK

In **Psalm 78,** at the beginning of the chapter, the psalmist is talking about David and mentions how David guided Israel. He mentions there were two characteristics in David that enabled him to do this successfully… a true heart and skillful hands. In our own self examination men, can we look at our marriages and our homes and identify some areas where we might be able to manifest these characteristics more strongly? What are those areas?

Identify three areas where men need to guide their families. Can you think of other areas as well?

Can you differentiate between how a husband may dominate his home and how he may guide his home?

Notice in **1 Peter** the wife is told to "fit in" with their husband's plans. Does that challenge you as a husband to come up with a plan for the family? Does that Scripture give you a deeper sense of responsibility toward the directions in which your family should take? How does it inspire you to be a better leader?

Chapter 3

H. *U.* S. B. A. N. D.

God has placed the husband in the home to be the **Head**. To fulfill this role effectively, he must **U**nderstand his wife's needs and desires. He is charged with **S**howing his wife and family what God looks like. He does this by reading the **B**ible daily. To maintain harmony and generate power, he seeks his spouses **A**greement for all decisions. Through love, he also **N**urtures his romantic relationship with her. As he becomes **D**iligent in his marital assignments, God can then bless this relationship.

U = Understand

1 Peter 3:7 NKJV *Husbands, likewise, dwell with them with understanding, giving honor to the wife, as to the weaker vessel, and as being heirs together of the grace of life, that your prayers may not be hindered.* Some translations use the word knowledge instead of understanding.

The world tells you that "Men are from Mars and women are from Venus." The world would tell you that it is impossible for men to understand women. But God!

God doesn't recommend, suggest or even intimate that men are to understand their wife. He COMMANDS us to understand our wife. And He doesn't expect us to do this from long distance either. He tells us to "Live with them according to knowledge and understanding." This is an up front, in your face, never leave you or forsake you kind of intimate relationship that He is talking about. Tim Taylor did not understand Jill Taylor. George Jefferson did not understand Weeze, but they are not our role models. God speaks to us clearly that we must live with our spouse and we must understand her. If this was impossible then God would not have commanded husbands to do it.

To Understand means exactly what it says. To "STAND UNDER."

When we take the time to listen to our wives and to empathize or really hear them, we are supporting them in their emotional needs. We are literally "standing under" them in a "support mode." The implication is clear, the more we live with them or the more we are around them, the greater opportunity we will have to understand them.

As someone who reads the Bible and attends Church and Marriage classes regularly, I am becoming successful in understanding Diane. There are many variables that go into the mix. There's an understanding what the Word of God says about wives. For example, because the Word of God tells me to love Diane as Christ loves the Church, I know now that I am filling her basic need in marriage as designed by God. When I couple that with the knowledge that I am the physically more dominant of the two, and add to that the fact that I am to serve her in love, I understand her need for the strength God has placed in me.

When I understand my role in marriage as head, I can now understand that God has placed in Diane a need and desire to follow that lead. All this information goes into the equation to help me understand the root motivators that are placed in Diane, enabling me to be a better husband.

U = Understand

When I understand that my wife has a "Task Oriented" personality as opposed to my "People Oriented" personality it diffuses the potential for friction that could result when these personalities clash in their desires. I no longer take offense when she is focused on a task and perhaps ignoring me in the process.

As I discover her "Love Language" I become better suited to understand the inherent need she has not only to be loved, but I understand how to fill that need specifically. Identified, I can now begin to accomplish that task more efficiently, and even understand why I am doing it

Galatians 6:7 NKJV ...*for whatever a man sows, that he will also reap.*

So according to this Scripture, if I sow understanding of my wife into my marriage, I can be confident that I can reap understanding from my wife in return. It's a two way street. Who among us husbands would not want to be understood also? That aspect alone could avoid many disagreements on down the road.

Proverbs 19:14 NLT ...*only the Lord can give an understanding wife.*

To Understand or to Stand Under is not just a "knowing something" word but it is a "doing something with what you know" word.

An important aspect of understanding that is often overlooked is that understanding usually is the impetus for service or action. Understanding is much more than just a nod of the head and a "Yup, I hear ya hon." That said, sometimes it is just a hug or shoulder rub. It took me over a decade to understand that lots of times Diane didn't want me to "fix" anything so much as she just wanted me to be there and listen to her.

MARRIAGE MAINTENANCE TRUTH
Understanding Hearts are Listening Hearts

Jesus understood our need for a redeemer. So He "STOOD UNDER" that need, did something about that need, gained mankind's favor, and now we love him unconditionally. The same thing will happen in our relationship with our wife. Men, if we will seek to understand our wives by standing under their needs and doing something to satisfy or meet that need, we too can garner unconditional love from them. God is so wise and so wonderful. He has created within our marriage so many ways, so many principles that lead us to achieve not only our desires and our goals, but His goal for us as well, to become ONE. We now know that by understanding our wives we can cause their love for us to blossom.

Rewards For Understanding

Proverbs 13:15 NKJV *Good understanding gains favor.*

Having a good understanding of my wife and her needs, wants and desires will reward me with favor from my wife. What man does not want or need more favor with his wife? Her outlook towards me will be favorable; her thoughts towards me will be favorable, resulting in her ultimately responding to me more favorably. I mean gee guys, for no other reason than that, we need to seek to understand our wife.

U = Understand

Proverbs 16:22 NKJV *Understanding is a wellspring of life unto him who has it.*

Wellspring implies a continual supply of something. It not only implies a continual source, but it is a well you don't have to dig. It is a well spring, meaning whatever is coming out of that well comes out on its own power. In this case, when we understand our wives this particular well that is springing up is giving us life. Not only does it give us life, but a continual supply of life, for my marriage. I would much rather have a continual supply of something good, something that brings life to my marriage, then to go from abundance to lack and lack to abundance again and again. The way we can insure that of happening is, understanding our wives.

I will grant you, most women are complex. I thank God Diane is complex, but my God is able to break down her complexities to me through me loving her, me serving her, me reading the Bible and me just living with her. God wants me to understand Diane. He has equipped us men with an ability to understand our wives, but we must learn to understand them on His terms. Why? Because when we use His way to do this, we are guaranteed that certain things will happen along the way that ultimately will lead to ONEness. God knows exactly what He is doing. Take His Word for it guys, follow the Scripture map and become all that you can be for your wife and for God.

Proverbs 5:15 & 18-19 NLT *Drink water from your own well – share your love only with your wife. Let your wife be a fountain of blessing for you. Rejoice in the wife of your youth. She is a loving doe, a graceful deer. Let her breast satisfy you always. May you always be captivated by her love.*

Other translations say:

The King James version – *Be ravished always with her love.*

The Amplified version – *Be transported with delight in her love.*

The New King James version – *Always be enraptured with her love.*

If that doesn't make you husbands want to understand your wife and have a wellspring of love in your marriage, we'll pray for you at the end of this chapter. It is important that we, as husbands, do all that is written in the Word. We should live with our wife with understanding in all areas, all the time. The promises from God are just so abundant. He offers us a well spring of life if we do this right. He promises us favor with her also. He says we can be captivated by her love. We won't have to force ourselves to love our wife, but we will be held captive by a love so strong that our relationship will wind up safe and on solid ground.

When we are "captivated" by something or someone, it means that we will not be able to be captured by something or someone else. We are already being held captive. When a man is captivated by his wife's love, he doesn't have to worry about going astray. He doesn't have to fear that he will have an affair. There is no possibility that that will happen… because… he is already being held captive and he cannot escape. Are you being held captive by the love you have for your spouse? Let those bars of love protect you from fooling around with other women. Let those bars of love keep you from entering places you shouldn't be entering. Let those bars keep your thoughts on your wife and on no one else.

U = Understand

Proverbs 3:13 NKJV *Happy is the man who finds wisdom, and the man who gains understanding.*

Who doesn't want to be happy? Here, God associates the finding of wisdom and the gaining of understanding with happiness. But look here at the process or the wording of this Scripture. We find wisdom and we gain understanding. The two are tied together, we must search for wisdom, but when we find it, we then gain understanding. Very rarely will one aspect of biblical truth stand alone. God has everything tied together for a purpose. It's all like a road map, or the Amazing Race. We discover one truth and it affects our lives and creates something else in us that will lead us to another discovery that produces more fruit. Here, we find wisdom and we then gain understanding which makes for a happy man. This is just one of many reasons to read the Word of God. Use this as an encouragement to get in the Word and dig out these truths. Be a prospector in the gold mine of God's Word and be a rich man indeed.

Sometimes we may need help concerning some of the deeper spiritual or emotional issues that may arise in marriage. We may feel we need specific help in trying to understand what is happening in our marriage. That's why we have Christian brothers and sisters. That's why we go to Church and create relationships with others. That's why we all should look closely at joining a life group or a home group. These are great places where we can have intimate discussions, and create relationships with other men that will allow us to safely talk to them. In our church we have a vital healthy men's ministry program. There is no shame in admitting we don't know it all.

Proverbs 11:14 NKJ *Where there is no counsel, the people fall; But in the multitude of counselors there is safety.*

That's why we read the Bible, so that we have resources that can help us to do a better job of understanding the true needs of our wife. We don't have to do this stuff alone. Marriage is the "Superbowl" that we live everyday. We need our "A" game every hour of the day to be successful. Take advantage of the resources that God puts in your path. Books like this one are helpful. Tap into the fullness of the Body of Christ and expect victory in every area of your marriage.

The Best Reward Of Understanding

1 Peter 3:7 NKJV *Husbands, likewise, dwell with them with understanding, giving honor to the wife, as to the weaker vessel, and as being heirs together of the grace of life, that your prayers may not be hindered.*

The best reward is the grace of life that is given to a married couple. What is the grace of life? I think it's like the icing on the cake or the cherry on top of an ice cream sundae. It's the over and above kind of life. It's the ability to live your life intimately with someone in the very presence of God. There is my relationship with God, then there is my wife's relationship with God, then, as we enter into the very best of God, it becomes OUR relationship with God.

The grace of life is the ultimate unification of that three-fold-cord. WOW!

Ecclesiastes 4:11-12 NLT *Likewise, two people lying close together can keep each other warm. But how can one be warm alone? A person standing alone can be attacked and defeated, but two can stand back-to-back and conquer. Three are even better, for a triple-braided cord is not easily broken.*

U = Understand

Never lonely, never alone, Diane, me and God working in harmony toward that ultimate goal… ONEness! Not only working, but enjoying each others company as we travel the road together. We celebrate our victories, sharing our setbacks; the three of us always in lock step, always on the same page. Diane and I are learning and growing together, not only with Him, but because of Him.

As believers, we are all given life. The Book of John tells us over and over again, *that whosoever believes* shall receive eternal life or everlasting life. Jesus says in

John 10:10 NKJV, *I have come that they may have life, and that they may have it more abundantly.*

But only to the husband and wife does it say that they can be heirs together of the GRACE OF LIFE.

That word Grace is the Greek word Charis. It literally means "the divine influence upon the heart and it's reflection in the life." Your Godly Marriage is not for just you alone. It's to reflect something. It's for the world to see the "ONEness" that is not only between a husband and a wife but the "ONEness" between God and us.

John 13:35 NKJV *By this shall all men know that you are my disciples, if you have love one for another.*

The other best reward is that your prayers are not hindered. In marriage, you have a built in "PRAYER PARTNER" with the "POWER OF AGREEMENT" at work.

Deuteronomy 32:30 NKJV *One can chase a thousand, and two can put ten thousand to flight…*

Ecclesiastes 4:9 LB *Two people can accomplish more than twice as much as one; for the results can be much better.*

Matthew 18:19 NKJV *Again I say to you that if two of you agree on earth concerning anything that they ask, it will be done for them by My Father in heaven.*

With that kind of power available in my marriage, I want to understand my wife so that the POWER OF MY PRAYERS ARE NOT HINDERED in any way, shape, or form. By doing this, God's way, I can be confident that God will be that triple-braided cord in my relationship with my wife.

TIME TO TALK

Understanding on the part of us men will require that we listen to our wives. How would you rate your listening skills? You can use a scale of 1-10 if that helps, ten being perfect.

We can even break down listening into many components. For instance, do we listen to our wives in certain areas, about certain things better than we do about other things? What are some areas where you would rate yourself a good listener to your wife? What are some areas where you think your listening skills need to improve?

This chapter mentions that sometimes when we seek to understand our wives it will require action on our part. Can you give an example when this was true in your home? What was your wife's response when you did this?

In **1 Peter 3:7** it says that when a husband lives with his wife according to knowledge and understanding they then have the ability to be "Partakers of the grace of life." What would you say *partaking of the grace of life* in your marriage would be like?

# Chapter 4

H. U. S. B. A. N. D.

God has placed the husband in the home to be the **H**ead. To fulfill this role effectively, he must **U**nderstand his wife's needs and desires. He is charged with **S**howing his wife and family what God looks like. He does this by reading the **B**ible daily. To maintain harmony and generate power, he seeks his spouses **A**greement for all decisions. Through love, he also **N**urtures his romantic relationship with her. As he becomes **D**iligent in his marital assignments, God can then bless this relationship.

S = *Show*

Husbands are also required to show their spouses and their family what God looks like. A man can't show... if he doesn't know. A husband shows that he knows by his actions or by his lack of action. It's not a matter of what a husband says but by what he does.

Hosea 6:6 LB *I don't want your sacrifices – I want your love; I don't want your offerings – I want you to know me.*

Colossians 1:10 NLT *Then the way you live will always honor and please the Lord, and your lives will produce every kind of good fruit. All the while, you will grow as you learn **to know God** better and better.*

Philippians 3:8 & 10 NKJV *Yet indeed I also count all things loss for the excellence of the knowledge of Christ Jesus my Lord, for whom I have suffered the loss of all things, and count them as rubbish, that I may gain Christ… that I may know Him and the power of His resurrection.*

Plain and simple, God wants us to know Him. Knowing God is a learning process and must become a priority in our life. Sin is a sure sign that we do not know God. Our lives will testify whether we know God or not.

1 Corinthians 15:34 NLT *Think carefully about what is right, and stop sinning. For to your shame I say that some of you don't know God at all.*

Titus 1:16 NLT *Such people claim they know God, but they deny him by the way they live. They are detestable and disobedient, worthless for doing anything good.*

In relating this to our jobs men, how many of us husbands go to work and we don't know what our assignment is? You can't do your job, if you don't know what your job is… and you can't follow your boss's orders, if you don't know him and you never talk to him.

Notice the task is to show them, it doesn't say to tell them, although we are to be speaking to our family about God continuously. It says to show them what God looks like. That means we live out our role as revealers of God by our actions. We live it out in thought, in word, and in deed.

Ephesians 5:25 LB *And you husbands, show your wives the same kind of love as Christ showed to the church when He died for her.*

S = Show

1 Peter 2:9 NLT *...for you are a chosen people. You are royal priests, a holy nation, God's very own possession. As a result, you can show others the goodness of God, for he called you out of the darkness into his wonderful light.*

God has called all of us to do this, to love, but in marriage it gains clarity and comes into focus as a man is charged with this particular task to a specific individual. Husbands say, "I don't know what God wants me to do"! Well here it is, start by showing your wife the *"same kind of love that Christ showed"* and then *"show them the goodness of God"* in you and through you.

This is another great place to begin. Show your mate the redemptive God at work in **your** life.

The Redemptive Names Of God

Jehovah – Jireh	**The Lord our Provider**
Jehovah – Shalom	**The Lord our Peace**
Jehovah – Shammah	**The Lord is Present**
Jehovah – Rophe	**The Lord our Healer**
Jehovah – Rohi	**The Lord our Shepherd**
Jehovah – Nissi	**The Lord our Banner**
Jehovah – M'Kaddesh	**The Lord who Sanctifies**
Jehovah – Tsidkenu	**The Lord our Righteousness**

Before we really get into this next part, let me assure you that we are not trying to deify husbands. If I as a husband am to *"love my wife as Christ loved the Church,"* then I should carefully look at in detail how Jesus loves. Jesus also tells us to follow His example in the things that we do, He laid down the pattern we are to follow. Paul tells us to be imitators of God.

John 13:15 NKJV *For I have given you an example, that you should do as I have done to you.*

John 13:15 MSG *I've laid down a pattern for you. What I've done, you do.*

Ephesians 5:1-2 NKJV *Therefore, be imitators of God as dear children. And walk in love, as Christ also has loved us and given Himself for us...*

Therefore, this is exactly what we intend to do in studying the Redemptive Names of God and how to apply that to us husbands in loving our wife and our children.

Jehovah – Jireh   The Lord Our Provider

For us husbands, that means we get up each day and go to work. We provide for our families in the same manner God provides for us. We show our families what a provider looks like.

Philippians 4:19 NKJV *And my God shall supply all your need according to His riches in glory by Christ Jesus.*

Jesus shows us the Father when He works. So too, can we husbands show the Father when we work. If it is good enough for Them, then it is good enough for us.

John 5:17 NLT *But Jesus replied, "My Father is always working, and so am I."*

Notice God always works. Working is one of the ways we imitate the Father. Husbands going to work faithfully paints a picture of God working, faithfully, on our behalf. It is so simple, this opportunity to preach a message to our wives and our children of who God is. Father God is a worker, and we show our family that aspect of the creator God when we go to work too.

John 10:38 NLT *But if I do His work, believe in the evidence of the miraculous works I have done, even if you don't believe me. Then you will know and understand that the Father is in me, and I am in the Father."*

Look at this. When Jesus did the work God assigned Him, He said that by working, people would realize that God was in Him. So... by us men working faithfully, it speaks as a witness that the Father is in us... especially as we show our wives what Jehovah-Jireh looks like.

John 14:10 NLT *Don't you believe that I am in the Father, and the Father is in me? The words I say are not my own but are from my Father who lives in me. And He does His work through Me.*

Jesus acknowledged that it was God who was doing the motivation, the ministry, and the miracles in Him. He just had to provide the earthly vessel.

Don't limit your "Jehovah-Jireh" thinking to you being a financial provider only. Yes, God commands husbands to be the financial provider.

1 Timothy 5:8 KJV *But if any provide not for his own, and specially for those of his own house, he hath denied the faith, and is worse than an infidel.*
Rather remember that we are to be doing all aspects of provision for our families.

For example, to blind Bartimeus, Jesus showed him that God would provide eyesight. To the host of the wedding party at Cana, Jesus showed him that God would provide wine. To Mary and Martha, Jesus showed them that God would provide life to Lazarus.

That means, we men, should be doing miracles in our homes as the needs arise. Let's get out of our boxes and into the supernatural. Jehovah-Jireh has provided for you the ability to show Him to your family by giving you a miracle working ministry just as He gave Jesus.

Just get your fleshly desires out of the way, quit being lazy or indifferent, get in the Word and let God live through you to your family. Watch what will happen when you do, husbands in their homes, working miracles, painting a picture of what God looks like by their actions. This is the Good News of the Gospel, lived right out in front of their wife and children.

Philippians 2:13 NLT *For God is working in you, giving you the desire to obey Him and the power to do what pleases Him.*

Philippians 1:6 NIV *Being confident of this, that He who began a good work in you will carry it on to completion until the day of Christ Jesus.*

I am sure this sounds intimidating to some, but you must know the Scriptures and what they say. God does not expect you to do this based on your own strength. Of course not, but He does empower you through the indwelling presence of His Holy Spirit. Then, as we submit to his leading we tap into that anointing which enables us to do this.

Think about it this way. Most of you guys have been going to work just about every day since you grew up. Now you know that it has been God enabling you to do it. It is He who gives you the strength every day to get out of bed when

S = Show

you don't feel like it, when you're sick, or when it seemed beyond your ability... but God is faithful! God begins HIS WORK in us and He will carry it on. Just get out of the way... and let Him.

Jehovah – Shalom   The Lord Our Peace

Husbands are to be an agent of peace in the home. We are to SHOW our families what God's peace looks like. We don't fly off the handle during times of adversity, but are always a stable, calming, peaceful presence in our homes.

2 Thessalonians 3:16 NLT *Now may the Lord of peace Himself give you His peace at all times and in every situation. The Lord be with you all.*

Wow!!!!!!! The Lord of Peace **HIMSELF** is bringing you peace. Other translations say, *"No matter what happens,"* or *"At all times and in every way."* Another says, *"Under all circumstances and conditions and whatever comes."* Therefore, peace is coming and you should be the agent on earth by whom it comes through as you show peace to your family.

Mark 4:37-39 KJV *And there arose a great storm of wind, and the waves beat into the ship, so that it was now full. And He was in the hinder part of the ship, asleep on a pillow: and they awake Him, and say unto Him, Master, carest thou not that we perish? And He arose, and rebuked the wind, and said unto the sea, Peace, be still. And the wind ceased, and there was a great calm.*

God is called the "Lord of Peace." Jesus is called the "Prince of Peace."

Isaiah 9:6 NKJV *For unto us a Child is born, unto us a Son is given; and the government will be upon His shoulder. And His name will be called Wonderful, Counselor, Mighty God, Everlasting Father, Prince of Peace.*

What is your family saying about you? Are you the agent of peace bringing calm to the storms of life, or are you the storm that they run and hide from. Once again, you don't have to **show** your family what Jehovah-Shalom looks like alone or by your own strength.

John 14:27 NKJV *Peace I leave with you, My peace I give to you; not as the world gives do I give to you. Let not your heart be troubled, neither let it be afraid.*

Jesus gives us all His peace. In its truest sense, "peace" is having a right relationship with God. Remember the angel came to Mary and said *"Peace on Earth, good will towards men."* The greeting was not to imply that there would be an absence of violence or unrest, but it was said to tell us that the way to God was opening again and we could enter into a relationship with Him through the soon coming sacrifice of Christ. It literally meant "Peace with God." It was God's offer of peace to us.

Actually, peace is the greatest manifestation of showing someone that we have a relationship with God. That is why it is so important that we stay tight with God. Our family is expecting leadership from us and part of that is showing them that we have a relationship with the Creator of all the earth. It is the absolute best position to lead from. We not only show our family we have a relationship with God, but as evidenced by our peaceful spirit, we show our family what He looks like.

S = Show

Husbands, are you offering "Peace with God" to your families? Is that invite out there every minute of every day? That angel came to a future wife and he came with an offer of reconciliation which would result in PEACE.

If we husbands truly want to represent Jehovah-Shalom to our families, we must institute reconciliation in the relationships in our home. Then, just as Jesus did, we come against the storms of life that may come upon us without a spirit of anxiety or fear. We then show our family peace by living in peace.

Jehovah – Shammah   The Lord Is Present

This is my favorite. I love this one. I think nowhere else does a man have a greater opportunity to show his family what God looks like than right here. Husbands are to be THERE for their families. The Lord is present, so then husbands must be present in the home. We are not talking about physically being there 24/7, but our hearts are there 24/7. Our family knows that they have access to us at any time just like they do with God. We are not running all over the place after our own pursuits. We are now married men and our first ministry, after God, is to our wife and children, in our home, serving our marriages at all times.

Perhaps one of our kids has a test that day. Dad can't be there because he has to work, but we let that child know that, "Hey, Daddy can't be there with you but know that come 10 o'clock when your test begins, I'll be praying for you." Maybe your wife has jury duty, we can't take off work, but we let her know that we'll be by to meet her at the court house for lunch. That's what I mean by being there 24/7. We have hearts of integrity towards our family and they know it because they see it demonstrated day after day, time after time.

Psalm 46:1 NKJV *God is our refuge and strength, a very present help in trouble.*

Look at this Scripture. When God is on the scene he becomes a place of refuge and He brings strength with Him. Guess what guys, you are no different. When you are on the scene you too should become a place of refuge for your families and you should also bring strength for them with you.

Are you beginning to catch this? The Bible says to be *"imitators of God"* **(Eph. 5:1 NKJV).** We as husbands imitate Him by acting like Him. If God is ever present, then bless God with everything that is in me, my heart and my spirit and as much as possible my body also, will be a very present help for my family. I will change my thinking. I will alter my schedule. I will look for opportunities where my family can see me in action. I will become a place of refuge for them. I will let them see my strength and allow them to draw on it.

Matthew 28:20 LB *... and be sure of this, that I am with you always, even to the end of the world.*

This was the promise that Jesus made to the church. Isn't that the same promise we made to our wife when we got married, till death do us part? That is why Paul can say this to us.

Hebrews 13:5 MSG *Since God assured us, "I'll never let you down, never walk off and leave you," we can boldly quote, God is there, ready to help.*

S = Show

Don't forget, we are loving our wives as Christ loved the Church. In this case, loving the Church means being with the Church... forever, never leaving or forsaking her. Well, then, I will forever be with my wife too!

John 17:24 NIV *Father, I want those You have given Me to be with Me where I am, and to see My glory, the glory You have given Me because You loved Me before the creation of the world.*

What a treat! Look at how Jesus phrased that... I WANT. That is awesome. Want implies desire. Jesus doesn't say need, He says WANT. Jesus is telling the Father that He WANTS YOU to be with Him.

That's my cue then. That is the example I show to my wife. I can best represent Jehovah-Shammah by SHOWING my wife that I WANT to be near her. Not coming home late from work. Not filling my day or night up with activities that will keep her from my side. A husband best shows his wife what Jehovah-Shammah looks like by letting her see that he wants to be near her.

Let's look at **Psalm 46:1 NKJV** again. Being a *"very present help"* means not only our bodies are there, but it also means our minds and our hearts are there. Not just present, but *VERY present.*

Look at what that very present help brings with it. It comes with refuge and strength. Isn't this wonderful, by us men being home spirit, soul, and body in times of need, we minister directly to our wives number one need... SECURITY. I'm telling you guys, God has pulled out all the stops in allowing us to show our wife and family what He looks like.

Jehovah – Rophe   The Lord Our Healer

The Lord who heals. God has chosen to reveal Himself to us through Jesus and His Word as a healer. While man in and of himself has no healing virtue or power, he still does get to represent God the healer to his wife and family just as Jesus did.

John 5:19 NKJV *Then Jesus answered and said to them, "Most assuredly, I say to you, the Son can do nothing of Himself, but what He sees the Father do; for whatever He does, the Son also does in like manner.*

Remember, Jesus told us He only did what He saw the Father doing. Likewise, we only do those things that we see Jesus doing. If He is our example and sets forth the pattern that we are to follow in loving our wife, and he brought forth healing, then get ready guys, God expects you to bring forth healing to your family.

Isaiah 53:5 NKJV *But He was wounded for our transgressions, He was bruised for our iniquities; the chastisement for our peace was upon Him, And by His stripes we are healed.*

The Amplified version adds *and with the stripes that wounded Him we are healed and made whole.*

In this Scripture, healing and wholeness are tied together. God as healer has made us whole from the damage of sin, iniquities, and the absence of peace. God as healer, not only heals our bodies, but in His wholeness, He heals our mind, our body, and our spirit as well. He is the all consuming God who brings wholeness to every aspect of our existence.

S = Show

WOW!!!!!! How in the world does a husband show that to his wife? First, remember that Scripture in **Galatians 2:20 NKJV,** *I have been crucified with Christ; it is no longer I who live, but Christ lives in me; and the life which I now live in the flesh I live by faith in the Son of God, who loved me and gave Himself for me.* It is suppose to be Christ living in you, and you live that out in faith. We are going to have to tap into the miracle power and presence of God. Remember what M. A. R. R. I. A. G. E. is –

Maintaining
A
Romantic
Relationship
In
A
Godly
Environment

It's in a Godly environment only that we can do this. We men are going to have to be like Jesus.

1 John 4:17 NKJV *because as He is, so are we in this world.* That is the truth, if you are in Christ.

2 Corinthians 5:17 NKJV *Therefore, if anyone is in Christ, he is a new creation; old things have passed away; behold, all things have become new. Now all things are of God...*

If the Word of God says you can do something, then you can do it by faith.

Mark 16:18 NKJV *... they will lay hands on the sick, and they shall recover.* How do you create the Godly environment in which to bring healing to your family?

Mark 1:35 NKJV *Now in the morning, having risen a long while before daylight, He went out and departed to a solitary place; and there He prayed.*

Jesus only did the things He saw His Father do.

John 5:20 NKJV *For the Father loves the Son, and shows Him all things that He Himself does; and He will show Him greater works than these, that you may marvel.*

Those works witnessed or showed people who God is.

John 5:36 NKJV *But I have a greater witness than John's; for the works which the Father has given Me to finish – the very works that I do – bear witness of Me, that the Father has sent Me.*

We are not only supposed to do them too, but we are to do even greater works.

John 14:12 NKJV *"Most assuredly, I say to you, he who believes in Me, the works that I do he will do also; and greater works than these he will do, because I go to My Father.*

No greater opportunity exists in life for miracles of healing than in a marriage where because of the love a man gives his wife, the atmosphere is primed for manifesting His presence. Jesus was moved with compassion before He did many of His miracles. We need to become compassionate as well as passionate towards our wife so that this same environment

S = Show

in which Jesus worked miracles, can be recreated in our homes.

God is love and He tells us over and over again that we need to love one another. But He goes out of His way to specifically command one class of people to love another. He makes a point to tell the husband that he is to sooooooo love his wife as Christ loves the church. Why???

Because outside of the sacrifice of the cross, no greater manifestation of love will ever take place than that which occurs when a woman places her life in the hands and heart of a man. And no greater love is needed to requite that commitment than the love God gives to a husband to do this, honoring him in the assignment.

Just like Jesus, if there is going to be any wounding going on in the relationship, I will take it. If there is any bruising occurring, let it be on me. I will imitate Christ the wounded, Christ the bruised and I will allow those scars to usher in healing for my relationship with my wife. Remember, as Christians when we get wounded we run to the healer. Learn to take those wounds in your relationship with your spouse, rather than giving them guys.

MEN, you must know Jehovah – Rophe intimately. You must know the healing love that comes from authority. You must know the miracle power that is available to you to show your wives the power that comes from the presence of God. We don't get to pick and choose how we will show God to our family. We need to show them the true God in the fullness of His character including – healing.

Jehovah – Rohi   The Lord Our Shepherd

Husbands are to show their wife and their family what the Shepherd looks like in the performance of all His duties. Jesus, always our example, is referred to as a Shepherd, three different ways.

1 Peter 5:4 NKJV *and when the Chief Shepherd appears, you will receive the crown of glory that does not fade away.*

Hebrews 13:20 NKJV *Now may the God of peace who brought up our Lord Jesus from the dead, that great Shepherd of the sheep, through the blood of the everlasting covenant,*

John 10:11 NKJV *I am the good shepherd. The good shepherd gives His life for the sheep.*

God may not have called us men to Pastor a church or lead a Bible study or even a home group, but we are charged with the welfare of a flock and that flock is our family. Truth is, we are actually Pastors in our home. We are shepherds to our families.

One of our most known and beloved Psalms is the **23rd Psalm (KJV)**. Here David, who himself is a shepherd, declares that *"The Lord is my Shepherd."* David knows from experience "in the field," what is involved with being a shepherd.

I shall not want. His sheep want or lack nothing because he knows he has provided everything they have need of or could want.

He maketh me to lie down in green pastures. His sheep are provided rest in a comfortable place as well as having a good food source. He knows sheep are very skittish and will only lie down if four things are met. Sheep must have freedom from fear, friction, pests and hunger. They don't just lie down in pastures, but they are green pastures. They are lush with vegetation.

He leads me beside the still waters. He knows that because of the bulkiness and thickness of their fur or coat, sheep have a natural fear of rushing and turbulent water. If a sheep were to fall in to the river, they would immediately sink. Also, because of the water weight of that sheep's coat, trying to get him out of the river would be near impossible.

He restoreth my soul. He knows that life is not always going to be this easy and quiet, but that there are hard places coming up ahead. He takes the time now to instill in them a sense of peace and security, not so much in where they are but in who they are with, their shepherd.

He leadeth me in the paths of righteousness for His name's sake. The shepherd's reputation is at sake here. If his sheep fall victim to the wolves, or are injured because of the harshness of the terrain, or if they starve because he did not provide for them, it is the shepherd's head that will roll with the owners of the sheep.

Yea, though I walk through the valley of the shadow of death, I will fear no evil: for Thou art with me: Thy rod and Thy staff they comfort me. He knows that even though the shepherd must take the sheep through those hard places and difficult situations sometimes, they will walk through and not stay in the valley. They will come out to the other side. He knows that the shepherd will stand his ground to protect those sheep, even with his very own life, and not cut and run from the peril. The shepherd's rod to protect and his staff to guide; which was also used to pull the sheep out of the thickets, was a symbol of comfort to the sheep.

Thou preparest a table before me in the presence of my enemies. He knows that even in the midst of enemies, the shepherd will prepare everything that those sheep need for that period of time. He prepares that table so the sheep focus and remember all that the shepherd has and will do for them and not look at what the enemy would try to do.

Thou anointest my head with oil: my cup runneth over. He knows the fear those sheep are experiencing when they see the enemy, so he takes the time to soothe them, assure them and comfort them. He builds their confidence up to overflowing by telling them that all is going to be all right. He handled the lion and the bear before. He can surely handle this enemy too.

Surely goodness and mercy shall follow me all the days of my life: and I will dwell in the house of the Lord forever. He knows that as a shepherd he must build that place of security for his sheep. That even in the event of the sheep wandering off, the goodness and mercy of the shepherd will follow after them and bring them back home.

As good as **Psalm 23** is, and as good as it paints the picture of what a SHEPHERD is and does, it only touches on what Jesus revealed to us about a truly Good Shepherd.

Jesus tells us husbands in **John 10:1-30** what the job of being a Good Shepherd entails. There are things that Jesus said about the shepherd and the sheep relationship that we as husbands representing Jehovah – Rohi need to implement in our homes.

John 10:2-5 LB *For a shepherd enters through the gate. The gatekeeper opens the gate for him, and the sheep hear his voice and come to him. He calls his own sheep by name and leads them out. After he has gathered his own flock, he walks ahead of them, and* *they follow him because they recognize his voice. They won't follow a stranger: they will run from him because they don't recognize his voice.*

John 10:27 LB *My sheep recognize my voice; I know them, and they follow me.*

The Shepherd is speaking and calling to those sheep. He is not silent and preoccupied with matters and distant from them. The Shepherd has spent time with those sheep and that is why they recognize his voice. Those sheep are not running from him but coming to him because he has built a good relationship with them. He walks ahead of them, making sure all is safe. Therefore, those sheep follow him because they know that good comes from following their shepherd.

In biblical times, when the shepherd would bring those sheep into the town or village square, as did the other shepherds, their sheep would all merge and mingle in one place. But because the sheep knew their shepherd's voice, when he would call to them, they would come out from amongst the other sheep and come straight to their own shepherd. The shepherd did not have to be concerned that his sheep would get lost amongst the other sheep and be lead astray by another shepherd.

John 10:9-10 LB *Yes, I am the gate. Those who come in through me will be saved. Wherever they go, they will find green pastures. The thief's purpose is to steal and kill and destroy. My purpose is to give life in all its fullness.*

One translation says, *"that they might have life and life more abundantly."* Green pastures. Have you given your family the comfort, rest and the provision they need? Here's a quick check for you husbands to see if you are fulfilling your role as a Good Shepherd. Are you giving life to your wife and family or are you stealing, killing and destroying your family with your harshness and abuse, or with your addictions and selfishness? People can read the kind of husband you are by the smile on your wife's face. Is your wife "smiling"?

> **John 10:11 *LB*** *I am the Good Shepherd. The good shepherd lays down his life for the sheep.*

Have you laid down your life, your wants and desires, to meet the need of your wife and family and what benefits the "Marriage"?

> **John 10:12-13 LB** *A hired hand will run when he sees a wolf coming. He will leave the sheep because they aren't his and he isn't their shepherd. And so the wolf attacks them and scatters the flock. The hired hand runs away because he is merely hired and has no real concern for the sheep.*

What kind of shepherd are you? Are you the fair weather kind? When trouble comes, do you go? Are you ready to jump ship when the storms of life come? Or, do you put on the armor of God and go to battle for your wife and family? Are the weapons of your warfare at the ready? Do you wrestle with flesh and blood (your wife and family) or against spiritual wickedness in high places?

> **John 10:14-15 LB** *I am the Good Shepherd; I know my own sheep, and they know me, just as My Father knows Me and I know the Father. And I lay down my life for the sheep.*

Over and over and over again Jesus is telling us that the GOOD SHEPHERD will lay down HIS life for THEIR life.

S = Show

The worthiness or the goodness of the sheep never comes into question when the subject of laying down his life for them comes in. Just because they are His, he willingly lays down HIS life for them.

John 10:27-29 LB *My sheep recognize my voice: I know them, and they follow me. I give them eternal life, and they will never perish. No one will snatch them away from me, for my Father has given them to me, and He is more powerful than anyone else. So no one can take them from me.*

When Jesus talked about "marriage," He said in **Matthew 19:5-6 KJV,** *For this cause shall a man leave father and mother, and shall cleave to his wife: and they two shall be one flesh? Wherefore they are no more two, but one flesh. What therefore God has joined together, let not man put asunder.*

That ties in with the role of the Shepherd. The Shepherd declares that his sheep *will never perish.* He declares that *no one will snatch them away from me.* Again he stresses the point that *no one can take them from me.* Husbands, are your wife and family being taken away from you because of the neglect you have shown them in not caring for them properly?

In **Deuteronomy 28:30 & 32 NKJV** under the curses that befalls a man who will not hearken unto the voice of the Lord his God and obey His commandments to do all, it says that, *You shall betroth a wife, but another man shall lie with her; you shall build a house, but you shall not dwell in it; you shall plant a vineyard, but shall not gather its grapes. ...Your sons and your daughters shall be given to another people, and your eyes shall look and fail with longing for* *them all day long; and there shall be no strength in your hand.*

So here is sort of a check list for you husbands. Have you provided a green pasture, a comfortable home for your wife and children? Comfortable doesn't have to mean expensive. Is it a place where they feel secure and safe because you are there? Security is not only a physical place; it can be an emotional place too. Have you provided that? Do your wife and children know your voice because of all the quality time you have spent with them? Has your voice inside their head ever stopped them from doing something that they shouldn't or urged them on to something great? Do they know by your words and your actions that you would lay down your life for them?

When you as a husband not only "TALK THE TALK BUT WALK THE WALK," you not only bring honor to your wife and family but you bring honor and respect to yourself. You become the Knight in Shining Armor who comes to rescue the fair maiden. Your praise will be spread abroad for all to see.

Jehovah – Nissi   The Lord Our Banner

Whether we admit it or not, whether we like it or not, there is a banner that is flying over our homes and hearts. Knights of Old and Lords of the Manor would fly a banner or crest over their castles. It showed whose it was and the crest would stand for something, usually a title, profession or it might even signify a special event that took place in the family at some point. The banner we fly is also a spiritual banner and may not be seen by man's eye, but angels and demons alike can see it and identify it whether for its strengths or its weaknesses and will respond accordingly.

S = Show

Psalm 60:4 NKJV *You have given a banner to those who fear You, that it may be displayed because of the truth.*

God has given you a banner. This is awesome in the **Harrison translation**.

Psalm 60:4 *"You have set up a standard for those who fear You, which they can rally around when hostile arms approach."*

That is a great picture of what a husband should be doing for his family when attacks or troubles come. Number one, as we represent "The Lord Our Banner" to our wives and family, we must remember we can show this banner because we live in and by the truth; the truth of God's Word to us and in us. The truth that says this is my family, they have been God gifted to me and I WILL guard and protect and lay down my life for them every minute of every day for as long as I live. No less a commitment will do!

Look at **Harrison's translation**... can your family "rally around you when hostile arms approach?" That is so awesome. Can they even find you when hostile arms approach? Are you bringing those hostile arms yourself? Tough questions guys, but you need to ask them of yourself and then allow God to grow you up and place you where you are needed in the home.

In the Kingdom of God, nearly everything is tied together. Remember, us men guarding our homes is part of our responsibility. When we do that, we unfurl the banner that will announce our intentions. What banner have you unfurled over your homes guys?

Song of Solomon 2:3-4 KJV *As the apple tree among the trees of the wood, so is my beloved among the sons.*

I sat down under his shadow with great delight, and his fruit was sweet to my taste. He brought me to the banqueting house, and his banner over me was love.

Husbands, do you see this? You are bringing your wife to a place of celebrating the marital covenant and the banner you are flying over your home declares your love for her. WOW!!!!!! Just take that thought home and chew on it for a while. Try to see yourselves and your marriage as it appears to others. Can they see that banner of love over your home? Is it tattered and worn, or is it lying on its side? Does it stand tall, proudly displayed by every thought, word and deed you do for your wife and family?

My wife has no concerns over the things I say about her when I am at work or with my friends. Course jesting, jokes or any other foul thing never comes out of my mouth at her expense. She's not my "old lady" or that "old battle ax." She is not my "ball and chain." She knows, because others have told her, how I brag on her all the time to them. There is not one person who knows me or who has spent time with me that doesn't know that "I love Diane." Everything I think or feel about her is said to all who are around me for I have raised that banner up high myself over her for all to see.

Here is another check list for you guys. What is the banner that is flying over your wife and your home saying to you neighbors and co-workers, family and friends?

Jehovah – M'kaddesh   The Lord Our Sanctifier

Jesus shows up in our lives as the "Sanctifier." Webster defines "sanctify" this way— "...to set apart as holy or for holy purposes, to consecrate, to purify or render sacred."

S = *Show*

Ephesians 5:25-26 NKJV *Husbands, love your wives, just as Christ also loved the church and gave Himself for her, that He might sanctify and cleanse her with the washing of water by the word.*

How does Jesus sanctify us? Let's look at **John 17:17 & 19 NKJV** to see what our example, Jesus does and use Him as our model. *Sanctify them by Your truth. Your word is truth. And for their sakes I sanctify Myself, that they also may be sanctified by the truth.*

So in other words, you can't give out what you don't have yourself. Jesus said that He sanctified Himself for our sakes so that He could affect us in the same manner. Then, that is what we husbands must do. We must sanctify ourselves so that we can affect our wives in the same manner Jesus affected the Church.

Why is sanctification so necessary for us? We started out talking about the ONEness which is the true God given reason why *"A man shall leave his father and his mother and cleaves to his wife and the two shall become ONE flesh"* **(Gen. 2:24 KJV).** Well, here in **John 17** Jesus is explaining what that **one**ness looks like and its purpose.

John 17:21-23 NKJV *that they may be one, as You, Father, are in Me, and I in You; that they also may be one in Us, that the world may believe that You sent Me. And the glory which You gave Me I have given them, that they may be one just as We are one: I in them, and You in Me; that they may be made perfect in one, and that the world may know that You have sent Me, and have loved them as You have loved Me.*

Jesus is not being redundant here because He has nothing else to say. He's trying to make a point that ONEness is the goal, it's the prize we seek to attain, and the reward we will share in is love. The God kind of love that the world can't give and the world can't take away.

Sanctification plays a big part in that ONEness process. It is God who makes us ONE. It is God who sanctifies us through Jesus and the work of the Holy Spirit and our obedience to Him. You cannot become ONE with your spouse without sanctification. ONEness is a holy place, it is a miracle of God that only He can give. But He requires sanctification as part of that process so that when we become ONE with our spouse it paints the picture of what a holy union with Him is supposed to look like.

> **Hebrews 13:4 NKJV** *Marriage is honorable among all, and the bed undefiled.* Other translations say *"the bed kept pure."*

> **Hebrews 13:4 MSG** *Honor marriage, and guard the sacredness of sexual intimacy between wife and husband.*

Don't let this stuff intimidate you guys. If Jesus did it for the Church through love, then it will happen to our spouses through love. It is just the natural progression of obeying God and leading a spiritual life that allows this to occur. I don't have to seek to sanctify Diane. I just have to love Diane. As I love Diane like Jesus loves the church, sanctification will be the result.

Jehovah – Tsidkenu
The Lord Our Righteousness

Time after time Jesus said that He and the Father were one... proof of relationship. No question, Jesus had the right to stand before God, in His presence, holy and righteous.

S = Show

Jesus is even called by such a name…

Malachi 4:2 NKJV *But to you who fear My name The Sun of Righteousness shall arise with healing in His wings;*

When the husband walks uprightly, hence righteously, the family can arise with healing and restoration. If we fear the name of the Lord, God promises that the Sun of Righteousness shall arise in our lives and He will bring healing with Him.

Think about some of the things that need healing in your home. Are there any relationships that need healing? Is anyone sick in the home? As leaders we need to invite the Righteousness of God into our homes and let His presence affect the entire family. The implication is clear in the above Scripture. When we fear God we will walk righteously and the presence of God will bring healing. I for one choose to walk righteously that my family may see God in all His righteousness as He comes into our home with the healing my family needs.

2 Timothy 2:22 NKJV *Flee also youthful lusts; but pursue righteousness, faith, love, peace with those who call on the Lord out of a pure heart.*

God tells all believers to pursue righteousness. In Marriage, husbands, wives and children are to pursue righteousness. But as men, husbands, leaders in the home, we have the unique ability to "set the tone" for this pursuit. Think about our own lives guys. How many of us are pursuing the same interests that our dad had? How many of us are golfers or fisherman because that is what Dad pursued. How many of us guys are working in the same fields that our dads worked? We need to give our children and wives a clear picture of the things they should be chasing after in this life.

God promises He will help us do this, but you have to want it guys.

Matthew 6:33 NKJV *But seek first the kingdom of God and His righteousness, and all these things shall be added to you.*

So many of us men, have lost the proper perspective concerning the priorities in our lives. They are God first, wife second, children third, job fourth and ministry fifth. Firstly, God not only says to seek the Kingdom of God, but He says to also seek the righteousness that goes with the Kingdom. To me, that means we are looking for God and His way of living too.

We are not just looking for someone, but we are looking for everything that is associated with that someone. In God's case, He chooses to tell us that righteousness is the thing that He wants to be associated with. Not only is righteousness the thing that He wants to be associated with, but it is the particular thing He wants us to pursue, or seek after once we come to know Him. We, as husbands, need to take the lead in this pursuit and show our families what a righteous God looks like.

TIME TO TALK

This chapter makes the statement that you can't show what you don't know. Name some of the ways you know will enable you to know God better.

I loved going through the redemptive names of God and then discovering how God has gifted man with the ability to

S = Show

show this aspect of God to his family. My favorite is Jehovah – Shammah, the Lord is Here or the Lord is Present. I liked it because it was something that I personally liked doing, being a refuge and strength to my family while always being available for them. What is your favorite guys, and why did you choose it?

What would be your wife's favorite and why would she choose that?

You must have noticed as you have read through this book that God's calling on you men is very demanding and it requires a great commitment and a spirit of excellence. But have you also noticed that He doesn't expect you to do this alone or by your own strength? Have you noticed that Jesus is always there as an example for you. Can you identify an area or two where you have not been doing these assignments with God, where you have been going it alone or perhaps, not going at all?

Would you also be willing to make a renewed commitment, right here, right now that you would "team up" with God and let Him live through you as He wishes so that you can truly show your family what God looks like? In your own words, alone, with your wife or someone else, verbalize that commitment.

Chapter 5

H. U. S. *B*. A. N. D.

God has placed the husband in the home to be the **H**ead. To fulfill this role effectively, he must **U**nderstand his wife's needs and desires. He is charged with **S**howing his wife and family what God looks like. He does this by reading the ***B**ible* daily. To maintain harmony and generate power, he seeks his spouses **A**greement for all decisions. Through love, he also **N**urtures his romantic relationship with her. As he becomes **D**iligent in his marital assignments, God can then bless this relationship.

B = Bible

Husbands are to be Bible readers. This is the starting point for everything we do in marriage, and in life. We must read the bible. It is our "supply line" for our faith, our wisdom, our ability, our strength, our peace, and everything else we choose to do.

Jesus is the head of the church, we need to check in with Him each day, (preferably each morning for starters) and get our marching orders.

Hebrews 1:3 NKJV *"...who being the brightness of His glory and the express image of His person, and upholding all things by the word of His power..."*

Jesus upholds all things by the Word of His Power. Your life, your existence, yes, even our marriages are being held together by the Word of His Power… or… by the power of His Word.

We need the power of God in our lives to be successful. The world comes at us at life speed. It catches us off guard, whether we are looking or not. As leaders in our homes men, we must have our defenses up against these problems and issues that will arise. We must be armed with answers when life's questions get tough. His Word will give us that. Not just wisdom, or insight, but His Word will provide us with the adhesiveness we need in our relationships. It's the ability to stay connected in tough times, especially to our spouses, even though they may be difficult to deal with at certain times.

I am convinced; there is no more powerful force in the universe than a man speaking the Word over his wife. We have the divine, supernatural connection that occurs in marriage. It's a holy connection and it consists of a three fold cord, God the Father, a husband and his wife. We have the life giving breath of God, the spoken Word of God in the mix. We add our faith to the Word we are speaking and there is not a demon in hell, not a worldly circumstance, not a fear or a disease that can withstand that supernatural combination.

Men, you want to see your wife blossom and bloom as never before, you get up in the morning or the middle of the night and you speak God's Word over her in her presence and I give you God's Word, your marriage will grow as never before.

Proverbs 2:6 *LB* *"For the Lord grants wisdom, His every word is a treasure of knowledge and understanding."*

B = Bible

God grants wisdom. Go get some. Where? *"His every Word."* I can probably number half a dozen areas where I need God's wisdom for something right now. I know what's good. I know what I should want. I feel I know what is best, and yet, I will not move without hearing from God's Word. I will wait patiently for His wisdom to manifest. I will read the Bible. I will pray the Bible. I will seek His face in the Bible and *He will perfect that which concerns me* **(Ps. 138:8 NKJV)**. That's just the way it is, that's just the way God does things. God grants wisdom with no strings attached. It is there for us to freely partake of.

God not only grants wisdom, but he tells us *His every Word is a treasure*. Not just a treasure, He then goes on to define what kind of treasure. It's a treasure of knowledge and understanding. Let's see, where have we heard that before? In **1 Peter 3:7** God told us husbands to live with our wives according to knowledge and understanding. Well, He just revealed here that His Word is a treasure of knowledge and understanding. I begin to see how God has crafted this whole life thing together. If we will just get in His Word, we will find the answers for everything we need.

I am a firm believer that God's Word, His wisdom and the power of His Word has an answer for every situation that will ever arise. I can be at odds with Diane over any number of things, and I can open the Word and find something that will apply. Diane and I may disagree over which car or house to buy, we may even disagree over whether to buy a car or a house. Then I read in **1 Corinthians 13:5** in many different versions, where God says that *Love does not insist on being right*, or *Love does not demand its own way*, or *Love doesn't insist on its own rights* and suddenly there is no more problem. The only "right" that I consider myself having in this marriage is the right to love Diane.

2 Timothy 2:15 KJV *Study to shew thyself approved unto God, a workman that needeth not to be ashamed, rightly dividing the word of truth.*

As much as we men may dislike school or studies, God commands us to study. I personally am uncomfortable in a controlled situation, forced to sit down and study, but it's my assignment and therefore it gets done. And don't forget, we are not being approved by man or even our spouse, we are wanting to be approved by God.

Remember, we have learned to study in school. We have been taught proper study habits so that we could pass a math or science class. Well, when we read God's Word we are studying life. We will be tested, not at some point down the road, but we are tested each and every day. We MUST know the answers.

We don't read the Bible like we read a novel or the newspaper. We will be taught by God's Holy Spirit to "rightly divide the Word of truth." Let me use my favorite Scripture to illustrate what I mean. It's **John 17:3 NKJV** and in my eyes there really isn't a more important Scripture in the Bible. *And this is eternal life, that they may know You, the only true God, and Jesus Christ whom You have sent.* Okay, let's "rightly divide" this Word of Truth.

Jesus is telling the crowd what eternal life is. I mean, WOW! If there is only one thing that anybody, anywhere, at anytime would tell me, the one thing that I would want would be how can I live forever! I mean, really, what else could surpass that! Jesus is going to tell us how to live forever. You ask most Christians what life eternal is and you would get many answers, but here, Jesus says you have to know and believe five things to live forever.

B = Bible

Number 1... we must know God
Number 2... we must know He is the ONLY TRUE God
Number 3... we must know Jesus... and Christ is not His last name, it's His title...
Number 4... we must know Jesus as the Christ, the Anointed One... the Messiah
Number 5... we must know He has been sent by God... He is God's only Messiah for us

That is how we are to read the Bible. Taking time, chewing on what God's Spirit is saying. And guys, be real, we break down the baseball box scores every day, we mull over our fantasy team selections. What sports fan doesn't know how many Super Bowls the Cowboys have won or who is the home run king? We know that stuff because we choose to take time and digest what facts we are handed. Now, we need to digest the Word of God as it's been written. Oh, by the way, when we get saved, God places the author of the book inside us. I mean, gee... how much simpler can God make it?

1 Peter 2:2 KJV *As newborn babes, desire the sincere milk of the word that ye may grow thereby.*

Ask God to change your desires if they are not right. Babies eat, if you are new at Christianity you need to eat also. If you are mature, you still need to eat. When we eat we grow. If our spirit man is not growing, it is because he is not eating. If you want to grow guys, if you want to grow into a mature Christian, a mature leader in you home, you will need to eat the Word of God. It's very simple, we would never starve our children or our wives, yet, so many of us men are starving ourselves.

Psalm 119:11 KJV *Thy word have I hid in mine heart, that I might not sin against thee.*

Sin problem men? READ THE BIBLE. God says that hiding His Word in your heart will cause you not to sin. How much simpler can He state it. If there is sin in our lives, we need to get in the book and allow the power of His word to affect us. This isn't rocket science, it is Christianity 101. Hiding the Word in our hearts releases us from the grip of sin.

Psalm 119:105 KJV *Thy word is a lamp unto my feet, and a light unto my path.*

Struggling for direction men? READ THE BIBLE. We hear this often too. Families are struggling for direction in their lives. Well, God has got that covered too. READ THE BIBLE. When I think about life and how the Word has been placed right in our laps by God, it becomes so clear and so simple. I don't understand why we fight against reading so much. I guess, actually I do. We have not put the flesh under where we tell it what to do and it doesn't tell us what to do. I guess that's why Jesus told us to be "disciples." That word means "discipline." Our flesh doesn't like that word, but that's too bad. Look at all the other disciplines we practice in our lives. We are disciplined in going to work, some of us work out, and we are disciplined in eating two or three meals a day. Why not just make a discipline of reading the Bible? It has far greater value than any other discipline that we will ever do.

John 15:7 KJV *If you abide in me, and my words abide in you, ye shall ask what you will, and it shall be done unto you.*

Aren't getting your prayers answered men? READ THE BIBLE. I just love this one. Jesus says, if you will abide or live in me… are you born again? Have you been washed in the blood of the Lamb? Are you saved? If you are, then the first part of this Scripture has been accomplished. Now the second part, does His Word live in you? That's on you guys. You must put the Word of God inside you and let it abide or live in you. Then you are promised that when you have met those requirements, then you can ask and it shall be done. There is no excuse for not getting your prayers answered.

2 Timothy 3:16 NKJV *All scripture is given by inspiration of God, and is profitable for doctrine, for reproof, for correction, for instruction in righteousness...*

That phrase, "given by inspiration of God" literally means it is "God Breathed." You should open up the Bible and it should be like "WHOOSH" the breath of God should greet you. You know, the only times I am close enough to my wife Diane to be under her breath is when we are having an intimate moment, whether it's sharing a kiss or a hug. It's the same way with God. You become intimate with Him when you read the Bible. But God brings a bonus when you are under "His Breath." That bonus is life.

In the Old Testament God picked up the dust of the ground and breathed onto it and LIFE came!

Genesis 2:7 NKJV *And the LORD God formed man of the dust of the ground, and* **breathed** *into his nostrils the breath of life; and man became a living being.*

Elisha, representing God, laid on top of the Shunammite woman's dead child's body, mouth to mouth, and life came!

2 Kings 4:32-35 NKJV *When Elisha came into the house, there was the child, lying dead on his bed. He went in therefore, shut the door behind the two of them, and prayed to the LORD. And he went up* *and lay on the child, and put his mouth on his mouth, his eyes on his eyes, and his hands on his hands; and he stretched himself out on the child, and the flesh of the child became warm. He returned and walked back and forth in the house, and again went up and stretched himself out on him; then the child sneezed seven times, and the child opened his eyes.*

In the New Testament, Jesus breathed over His disciples and the life of the Holy Spirit came.

John 20:22 MSG *Then he took a deep breath and breathed into them. "Receive the Holy Spirit," he said.*

When you are under the breath of God, life comes. That is why all Scripture is profitable, God breathes His life into it. The Bible says that God's Word is profitable to you in four ways:

#1 The Word of God is profitable for doctrine. This is a moral code by which you will base your actions upon. For instance, in my home, we do not curse, and we do not watch "R" rated movies. We don't belittle one another, we do go to Church, and we do help each other. This is part of the doctrine which we have created for our home through the Word. There is much more to it, but we stick to the Word as closely as possible when creating our doctrine, the moral code we will live by.

#2 The Word of God is profitable for reproof. When I was growing up we had a co-worker or a fellow student proof read our reports. Just in case we made a mistake, they would spot it and point it out to us. The Word of God does that now. He will proof read your life. He will point out the errors, if there are any; sort of like a spiritual spell check.

#3 The Word of God is profitable for correction. The Word of God will not only proof read us, but He will also make the necessary corrections.

#4 The Word of God is profitable for instruction in righteousness. That's neat. Basically it means that we will be structured or built up in righteousness. What the Word will do is simply build us up to look like God. You can't be *"an imitator of God"* without the Words of God working in you.

The importance of reading the Word daily cannot be over-emphasized. The Word is our life's blood to everything we will ever do in the Kingdom of God. You will not be able to love God as you should if you don't read the Bible. Your love for God will make you want to read the Bible. The more you read the Bible the more you will love God.

Men don't read the Bible because: **#1** Too Busy, **#2** Too Lazy, **#3** Don't Like to Read. If that is you, get the Bible on CD's. The new dramatization versions are awesome.

Deuteronomy 8:3 NKJV & Matthew 4:4 NKJV
"Man shall not live by bread alone, but by every word that proceeds out of the mouth of God."

Men, if you need three meals a day of food then you should need three spiritual meals a day from the word of God much more. Instead of the breakfast of champions, how about sitting down tomorrow, opening up His book and have breakfast with the CHAMPION.

TIME TO TALK

I know some men don't like reading. It's just not in them to read. But did you know there are other ways that you can invest Scripture inside you? Discuss some of those ways and see if one of them may appeal to you.

When we become Christians we are born again and we are actually called "baby Christians." Like all babies, we have needs. One of the surest signs that we have become "born again" is our need to eat and what we eat is "spirit food." Jesus said in **John 6:63 NKJV,** *"...the words that I speak to you are spirit and they are life."* Talk among yourselves about your personal eating habits and see if you are getting enough "spiritual nourishment." You may discover an idea that will help you in your effort to grow spiritually.

God says in **Proverbs 2:6 LB,** *He grants wisdom... His every Word is its own treasure of knowledge and understanding.* Take inventory of your life today guys, can you think of an area where you could use some of God's wisdom?

Timothy writes that all Scripture is "God Breathed" and is profitable for you. What other things in your life would you say are profiting you right now to become the husband God and your wife need you to be? Make a list and show it to your spouse.

Now make a list of things that perhaps are not profiting you, but are actually taking away or depriving you from becoming the husband God and your wife need you to be. Not only share that list with your spouse but you may want to see if she has anything to add to it!

Chapter 6

H. U. S. B. A. N. D.

God has placed the husband in the home to be the **H**ead. To fulfill this role effectively, he must **U**nderstand his wife's needs and desires. He is charged with **S**howing his wife and family what God looks like. He does this by reading the **B**ible daily. To maintain harmony and generate power, he seeks his spouses **A**greement for all decisions. Through love, he also **N**urtures his romantic relationship with her. As he becomes **D**iligent in his marital assignments, God can then bless this relationship.

A = Agreement

> **Luke 22:20 NLT** *After supper he took another cup of wine and said, "This cup is the new covenant between God and his people—an agreement confirmed with my blood, which is poured out as a sacrifice for you.*

MARRIAGE MAINTENANCE TRUTH
Agreement Is The Place Of Power
In A Marriage

Quite often in Scripture the word "Agreement" is used to clarify the word "Covenant." It immediately follows the word "covenant" in numerous Scriptures, as a means of further explaining what a covenant is. While succeeding in helping us to understand what a covenant is, using the word "agreement" in this manner also helps us to understand the power that is associated with the word "agreement."

> **Matthew 18:19 NKJV** *Again I say to you that if two of you agree on earth concerning anything that they ask, it will be done for them by My Father in heaven.*

Further biblical explanation of how powerful agreement can be is right here in Jesus' statement to the crowd. Look at the separate thoughts Jesus talks about here and then let's see how this applies in marriage. He says *"if two of you."* That's great, that means my wife and I can do this agreement thing. He says *"If two of you will agree."* We can agree. The question always is, will we agree? Matter of truth, we agree quite often. It just seems that the disagreements get most of the attention.

He states that *"if two of us agree on earth."* Okay, that means Jesus is talking to people here on the planet Earth, those of us who are alive here today. Wonderful, that's still me and my wife. Next is *"Anything they ask."* Right here He reminds us to pray. So for starters, we can look at this as a prayer Scripture. He is encouraging us to come together and agree in prayer. All of us couples should be able to do this. Next, He reveals His Father's promise. Our Father's promises that if we will do this… *"it will be done for them by My Father in heaven."* The Scripture doesn't say, "it might be done, or could be done, or hopefully will be done." The Scripture says *"It will be done."*

So, let's look at the qualifications again for this availability of power to manifest in our lives. The ingredients are:

A = Agreement

Two of us
    Agree
        Alive on Earth
            Asking Anything
                Asking the Father

I believe those ingredients are found in just about every home in married life. Well then, what's keeping us from doing this? We need to hone in on the promise... *IT WILL BE DONE*. Let's not shy away from the promises of God just because we think they are so great.

Numbers 23:19 NKJV *God is not a man, that He should lie, Nor a son of man, that He should repent. Has He said, and will He not do? Or has He spoken, and will He not make it good.*

Webster defines "agree" as "to come in to or to be in harmony."

Amos 3:3 NKJV *Can two walk together, except they are agreed?*

In marriage we are to be in harmony. If we are not currently in harmony we need to begin the process of "coming into harmony." The above Scripture is quite clear. How can you walk out this life together if you are not in agreement, not in harmony? It will make for a rough road to travel without this harmony, plus, we are denying ourselves the place of power as designed by God for our marriage.

Leadership means it is us guys who will make sure that this agreement is paramount in our relationship with our wives. We may have to take the "low end," we may have to use our leadership to be the first to humble ourselves, but that is what true leadership is all about.

MARRIAGE MAINTENANCE TRUTH
In God's Kingdom, Leadership Takes The Low End

I would rather come off my position and find the place of agreement with my wife and have the presence of God involved, than be right, wound my wife and not have the presence of God. God cannot bless strife, actually the Scripture says in **James 3:16 KJV**, *"For where envy and strife is, there is confusion and every evil work."*

Let us not forget either, that once we come into agreement, the place of power, the partner who may have given in must make it an unqualified agreement. That is, they are willingly sacrificing their position for the sake of harmony. They do this with no recriminations. They get on board with the others plan totally. What this does is remove backbiting down the road if it turns out that they made a wrong decision. It removes the "I told you so" from the discussion.

In my home, it is usually me who will give in. It doesn't bother me at all. I am not compromising my beliefs or my headship responsibilities. Personally, I think it is a sign of my growing as a leader. God always shows up whether we have made the right decision or the wrong decision, because His Word promises He will. In that place of agreement, that place of power, if we are on the wrong path, if we are ready to make the wrong decision, God usually shows up to correct the mistake before it happens. That would not happen if we were in disagreement or strife.

Mark 3:25 NKJV *And if a house is divided against itself, that house cannot stand.*

The Message version – *A constantly squabbling family disintegrates.*

A = Agreement

The New Living version – *a family splintered by feuding will fall apart.*

The Living Bible version – *A home filled with strife and division destroys itself.*

We have all heard this Scripture before. This is the penalty for not walking in agreement. We not only lose the opportunity to exhibit the power that we need to do marriage successfully, but we skip right past neutrality and go straight to destruction. If you and your wife are not living in agreement you run the risk of causing the fall of that marriage and its destruction.

We have many, many opportunities to come into agreement with each other each day and throughout each week. We need to find common ground in our relationship so we can enter this place of power. Remember, marriage is a trinity relationship between a husband and a wife and their God. The common ground in marriage should always be God and His Word. He is the Rock, He is our center. His Word is our "Moral Compass," if I may borrow a phrase. We don't invite God into our lives to conform to us, but we allow God's Holy Spirit to conform our lives to His Word.

Matthew 19:6 NKJV *So then, they are no longer two but one flesh.*

The goal in marriage as defined in **Matthew 19:5 NKJV** is ONEness. And Jesus said, *'For this reason a man shall leave his father and mother and be joined to his wife, and the two shall become one flesh'*. Actually, the above Scripture doesn't even state ONEness as a goal, but rather as a truth. Well then, all the more reason to maintain harmony and agreement in the home.

Isaiah 1:18 NKJV *"Come now, and let us reason together," says the Lord.*

God takes the lead in finding a place of agreement with us in our relationship with Him. There's our example. If God can take the lead and find common ground with His own, so too can a husband. Sometimes seeking agreement with my wife may force me to humble myself or sacrifice my position. Isn't that what Jesus did?

Philippians 2:5-7 NLT *You must have the same attitude that Christ Jesus had. Though He was God, He did not think of equality with God as something to cling to. Instead, He gave up His divine privileges; He took the humble position of slave.*

Matthew 23:12 NLT *But those who exalt themselves will be humbled, and those who humble themselves will be exalted.*

God will always take care of those who honor His Word. You and your spouse can always agree on the Word of God no matter what the disagreement is all about. You are not really giving up anything at all when you decide to "give up" something in order to find that place of agreement with your spouse.

If, I, as a man will read the Bible and allow for God's wisdom through His Word to be the source for my thinking, then I will not be asking my wife to agree with me so much as I will be asking her to agree with God's Word. It then becomes incumbent upon me to know God's Word and choose to go there when disagreement comes.

If, I, as a man will pray when disagreement comes with my wife and seek God's will, my wife will see my heart in the matter and God will be able to speak to the one of us

A = Agreement

who might be in error. It is my job to lead in this manner. But if I don't care what God says, then I am not looking for agreement, but self-gratification. I am insisting on having my own way... not God's.

Sure, we as men get to make the final say in decisions where we might disagree about something, but it doesn't have to be done with a heavy hand or in strife. It can be done with your wife trusting your decision because of your attitude of service towards the marriage. Most disagreements come when one person is defending their own rights.

1 Corinthians 13:5 NLT *Love does not demand its own way.*

Agreeing to disagree is a violation of the Word and destroys unity. God's way is better.

Romans 12:10 NKJV *Be kindly affectionate to one another with brotherly love, in honor giving preference to one another.*

Romans 12:10 MSG *Love from the center of who you are; don't fake it. Run for dear life from evil; hold on for dear life to good. Be good friends who love deeply; practice playing second fiddle.*

Ephesians 4:3 AMP *Be eager and strive earnestly to guard and keep the harmony and **one**ness of and produced by the Spirit in the binding power of peace.*

If there is power in agreement, then why would I be willing to **DIS** the **POWER** by **DIS**ing the **AGREEMENT.**

Look at how powerful agreement can be from God's point of view. God Himself had to break the power of agreement when the tower of Babel was being built. God had to send confusion to them to break their agreement.

> **Genesis 11:6 NLT** *"If they can accomplish this when they have just begun to take advantage of their common language and political unity, just think of what they will do later. Nothing will be impossible for them!"*

This principal applies to us in marriage also. If we can come to the place of common speech and unity, saying the things that God has said about us and walking in the power of agreement in our decisions, there is nothing we cannot accomplish together. When we agree with God and His Word, when we allow God to act as the umpire, casting the deciding vote in the decisions that we need to make, not only will we stay out of disagreement, but we will stay in the place of power and there will be peace in our home.

> **Colossians 3:15 AMP** *And let the peace, the soul harmony which comes from Christ, rule and act as umpire continually in your hearts, deciding and settling with finality all questions that arise in your minds.*

As head of home, it is the man's responsibility to find "thus Saith the Lord" in the Bible to help in situations where there may be disagreement. If he fails to do that, then the task falls on the wife who then is charged with the task of kindly instructing her husband with the Word. Don't you just love that phrase there; soul harmony. Harmony of souls, that's what agreement offers us.

As Christians (which literally means "Little Christ") the Word of God should be the ultimate source for our wisdom and knowledge. We don't argue with the Word, we are to just obey the Word.

James 3:17-18 LB *But the wisdom that comes from heaven is first of all pure and full of quiet gentleness. Then it is peace-loving and courteous. It allows discussion and is willing to yield to others; it is full of mercy and good deeds. It is whole hearted and straight forward and sincere. And those who are peacemakers will plant seeds of peace and reap a harvest of goodness.*

Look at the power in the negative available to Adam and Eve in the Garden of Eden. They agreed with the enemy that God lied. They were in agreement to disobey and they received the ultimate dishonorable miracle, salvation lost for mankind.

Look at the power in the positive available to Christ in the Garden of Gethsemane. He was struggling, yet He said, I agree with the Father's will for my life, and then the greatest miracle was prepared for, salvation for any and all.

This doesn't have to be so "spiritual" either. Simple everyday decisions like school, finances and job related issues will require agreement also. Remember, practice agreement with your wife, don't make a move without coming to God and His Word and to that PLACE OF POWER.

TIME TO TALK

Agreement allows both husband and wife to experience first hand, up close and personal, the presence of God through the manifestation of His power. Think back to an issue where you and your spouse were in agreement and detail how things went.

As a husband it is my place to insure that we are coming into agreement in critical areas. We are not puppets and we don't have to agree on every little thing, but we need to adopt an attitude of guarding the agreement process in our marriage. What are some things that I as a husband must do to insure this?

Marriage is a trinity relationship between a husband and a wife and their God. This agreement principle includes making sure that God's voice is heard. In your home, who usually initiates the idea that we will include God in this discussion? How is that done?

Knowing that you are called to lead, husbands, and knowing that ultimately it will be you who must use your authority by perhaps being the first to give in to maintain harmony and avoid conflict, how does that make you feel? Do you feel frustrated or does taking the low end give you a sense of fulfillment and empowerment?

Chapter 7

H. U. S. B. A. N. D.

God has placed the husband in the home to be the **Head**. To fulfill this role effectively, he must **Understand** his wife's needs and desires. He is charged with **Showing** his wife and family what God looks like. He does this by reading the **Bible** daily. To maintain harmony and generate power, he seeks his spouses **Agreement** for all decisions. Through love, he also **Nurtures** his romantic relationship with her. As he becomes **Diligent** in his marital assignments, God can then bless this relationship.

N = *Nurture*

God has also given the man the responsibility of nurturing romance in the home. Man has a great desire for sexual intimacy. He can either honor that desire God's way or fulfill his desire in a counterfeit manner, which is the way the world operates. Understanding the sexual relationship can help cultivate the heart of a "nurturer" in man concerning romance.

Let's put it this way. This is something I heard from one of the couples that we minister with at Lakewood. They were teaching the pre-marital class there and it really caught my attention. She said, "Concerning sexual gratification, man has the need and woman has the gift." I had never heard it put like that before, but I like it a lot. Sexual gratification for the husband has been placed in his wife as a "gift." If we husbands will remember that when we approach our wives, I believe it would heighten our sensitivity in this area.

Romance is the process that leads to a husband fully enjoying the gift of sex which God has placed in his wife. Nurturing Romance is the attitude that begins and completes this process.

MARRIAGE MAINTENANCE TRUTH
Everything A Husband Does Either Nurtures Or Detracts From Romance

Romance is defined by Webster as "A kind of love between the sexes... characterized by high ideals of purity and devotion, strong ardor..."

The husband nurtures this romance by letting his wife see and hear his devotion to her. In **Song of Solomon** the young man tells his lady he loves her... he tells her she is beautiful. He goes into a very descriptive dialogue with her which sets the tone of their physical relationship.

We as husbands need to remind our wives that we love them, EVERY DAY. We need to remind them that they are beautiful. We remind them not only by telling them but by showing them as well! Romance is:

> **R**emembering
> **O**ur
> **M**ates
> **A**lways
> **N**eed
> **C**lose
> **E**ncounters

N = Nurture

Proverbs 5:15 & 18-19 NLT *Drink water from your own well—share your love only with your wife. Let your wife be a fountain of blessing for you. Rejoice in the wife of your youth. She is a loving deer, a graceful doe. Let her breasts satisfy you always. May you always be captivated by her love.*

The Living Bible version – *let her love alone fill you with delight.*

The New American Standard Bible version – *Be exhilarated always with her love.*

The Amplified version – *always be transported with delight in her love.*

The King James version – *and be thou ravished always with her love.*

The English Standard version – *be intoxicated always in her love.*

The New King James version – *And always be enraptured with her love.*

Husbands, if you cause your wife to know that this is how you feel about intimacy with her, sharing intimacy with her will never ever become a problem in your relationship with her. There are other ways of securing your physical intimacy with your wife and nurturing romance.

Proverbs 19:22 *LB* *"Kindness makes a man attractive."*

The New King James version – *What is desired in a man is kindness.*

The Amplified version – *That which is desired in a man is loyalty and kindness.*

The New Living Translation – *Loyalty makes a person attractive.*

The English Standard version – *What is desired in a man is steadfast love.*

Start "wooing" your wife guys by acts of kindness and loyalty. Don't forget, nurturing is a process. In marriage it becomes a lifelong process. Your "six pack" may last for just so long, but your kindness and loyalty can last a lifetime.

Your task is to make a connection with your wife that allows you to have your need for physical intimacy fulfilled while meeting her need to have a strong emotional/spiritual connection. As leader in the home the job falls on you to discover how to accomplish this and then create a way to achieve it.

No books will be written that will help you discover your spouse's very specific need. It is part of the process of becoming one that is so challenging and rewarding at the same time. Marriage is all about discovery and as you intentionally nurture your wife's need for this connection… which is called "romance" you will discover a deeper meaning of love that will give you a greater understanding of who she is. There can be great joy in the learning process if you handle it correctly, by giving instead of getting.

The number one trait women want to see in their man is… spirituality or spiritual leadership. Understand this men, just as you have a need/desire/hunger for sexual gratification,

N = Nurture

God has placed the same need/hunger/desire inside a wife. But her desire is not for sex, it is to see you fulfilling your headship duties. It is the need to have you being the spiritual head of your home by leading in prayer, worship and Bible reading. It is you, ushering in the presence of God in difficult situations. As often as you think about sex and your need, you need to recognize your wife's desires and her needs too.

Genesis 3:16 AMP *To the woman He said, I will greatly multiply your grief and your suffering in pregnancy and the pangs of childbearing; with spasms of distress you will bring forth children. Yet your desire and craving will be for your husband, and he will rule over you.*

MARRIAGE MAINTENANCE TRUTH
If God Has Called The Husband To Lead, He Has Then Called The Wife To Follow That Lead

As surely as night follows day, wives are made to follow their husbands lead. Wives have been called by God to see husbands lead their homes and to willingly follow that Godly leadership. The most powerful way that we men can "Nurture Romance" in our homes is to let our wives see God living in us. If we think it through, it will be plain to see.

God's love to us is what won us to him. Actually, the model of how ONEness works in the kingdom is shown right here. The Bible says *"God so loved"* **(John 3:16 NKJV)**. There is the Love component that husbands are to have with their wife. The Bible also says in **Romans 5:8 NKJV,** *God demonstrates His own love toward us, in that while we were still sinners, Christ died for us.* There is the Honor/Respect component that wives are to have with their husband. It was this Love/Honor dynamic that caused us to respond to Him.

In His ultimate wisdom he put that Love/Honor dynamic in the marriage. He created man with a deep need to be honored and respected and he created woman with just as deep a need to be loved or made to feel secure. The purpose of God loving us and honoring us was to bring us into a relationship with Him that results in ONEness. It worked. So He put the same dynamic into marriage, wives honoring and respecting their husbands, husbands loving and making their wives feel secure. It works here too; the result is the same, a relationship resulting in ONEness.

When wives see the husband doing what he is supposed to be doing... Loving them, causing them to feel secure, leading their home spirit, soul, and body, its causes them to have feelings of ardor for their husbands. Ultimately, that is how we nurture them. We don't nurture romance in our wives by giving them something they have no need of. We nurture romance in our homes by filling their deeper needs. Their number one need is to fill that leadership void in their lives.

Don't forget, God did not tell the wife to lead the home. So, unless we men do it, that void remains and wives go through life unfulfilled. Flowers and candy are nice guys, but just do what you are called to do and everything else will fall into place. I give you God's Word on it!

TIME TO TALK

Okay guys, sensitivity training 101, here it comes. Look back on your day or recent days and recall your desire for physical intimacy. Now, go back in that day and try to recall how you were ministering to your wife's need for romance.

N = Nurture

Can you see how "nurturing romance" is a full-time job? Can you now understand that God has created your wife totally differently than the way He created you? In order for you to have a physically intimate life with your wife, you will need to meet her need for emotional intimacy. What are some ways you can meet her need for that emotional intimacy she so desperately requires?

There are lots of things that we husbands do that help meet this need in our wives. Talk about some of your efforts and then listen to her as she lets you know whether she feels the same way about them as you do. This should be interesting, even if your wife doesn't see your efforts as successful, the conversation alone should get you started well on the way towards learning how you can meet those needs

Chapter 8

H. U. S. B. A. N. *D*.

God has placed the husband in the home to be the ***H*ead**. To fulfill this role effectively, he must ***U*nderstand** his wife's needs and desires. He is charged with ***S*howing** his wife and family what God looks like. He does this by reading the ***B*ible** daily. To maintain harmony and generate power, he seeks his spouses ***A*greement** for all decisions. Through love, he also ***N*urtures** his romantic relationship with her. As he becomes ***D*iligent** in his marital assignments, God can then bless this relationship.

D = **Diligent**

Proverbs 22:29 KJV *Seest thou a man diligent in his business? He shall stand before kings.*

If we can take anything from the previous sections in the book, it must be that God has challenged husbands with the task of excelling in our marriages. It's a privilege and a responsibility at the same time. It's sweat and it's reward. It's failure and it's victory. It's joy and it's sorrow. But it is all in the perfect will of God and we need to pay attention and do our best in all of the afore mentioned situations. Marriage is THE BUSINESS of the Husband, especially a new husband. That is why when a young man first gets married, he is to take one year off from work or war in order to secure the foundation of his relationship with his wife.

Deuteronomy 24:5 NKJV *When a man has taken a new wife, he shall not go out to war or be charged with any business; he shall be free at home one year, and bring happiness to his wife whom he has taken.*

The focus or the diligence of the newly married husband is *bringing happiness to his wife.* We can expect God to exalt that husband as he proves diligent and dutiful in his responsibilities.

Proverbs 12:24 NKJV *The hand of the diligent will rule, but the lazy man will be put to forced labor.*

One of the meanings in Strong's Concordance for the word "diligent" is "gold" as in "gold that is mined." That paints a great picture of the effort and determination we husbands should be exerting in doing our marriage assignment.

Proverbs 12:24 MSG *The diligent find freedom in their work; the lazy are oppressed by work.*

What a great promise as well as a great warning. There is freedom for us husbands to live out our marriage responsibilities when we are diligent. No one wants their marriage to be a chore. Well, the Word says it doesn't have to be. There is freedom in marriage for the diligent husband. Conversely, when we are not diligent, the marriage can become a burden, or it can be oppressive. The choice is ours. Will we be diligent in the business of marriage, or will we leave it on "auto pilot" and watch it run out of gas and crash and burn. You can be diligent in your marriage responsibilities and leadership role willfully, joyfully, and under God's gentle guidance... or it can become a forced trial in your life.

D = Diligent

The choice is yours. Look at some of the promises from God concerning the "Diligent" man before you make your decision.

Proverbs 12:27 NIV *The lazy man does not roast his game, but the diligent man prizes his possessions.*

A quick self-check here to see if you are diligent. Do you prize your wife and your family? Do you set your marriage up high on a pedestal as a God given gift? Do you honor your vows and commitments to the marriage? Are you speaking and acting accordingly, recognizing your wife and children as prized possessions gifted from God **OR** are you like that lazy man, never enjoying what God has given you?

Proverbs 13:4 NIV *The sluggard craves and gets nothing, but the desires of the diligent are fully satisfied.*

Another self-check, are you satisfied? Are you satisfied that your marriage is on the right track? I don't mean do you consider it the "perfect" marriage. What I mean is, is your marriage growing and do you feel fully satisfied? Am I growing as an individual? Is my wife growing? Of course we can still do better, but if we are diligent in our marriage then we can rest assured knowing that we are in the center of God's will. Coming seasons are full of promise and hope for our lives, **OR,** is nothingness filling your marriage and the empty feelings it brings with it.

Proverbs 21:5 NIV *the plans of the diligent lead to profit.*

As I read through these Scriptures, it never fails to astound me how simple and practical, yet profound and powerful the Word of God is. If one is diligent, that diligence will lead to profit. If one is diligent in marriage, then that diligence will lead the marriage to profit. How does a marriage profit? It profits when the husband and wife fulfill God's plan for their lives by becoming ONE. It profits when the marriage is used to be a witness for the Kingdom of God. It profits when the children are being raised in a household where the husband is diligent and they are being raised in the nurture and the admonition of the Lord.

2 Timothy 2:15 NKJV *Be diligent to present yourself approved to God, a worker who does not need to be ashamed, rightly dividing the word of truth.*

Any shame about the job you guys are doing in your marriage? Are you able to come before God and show Him the effort you have made in your marriage? We stand before God when it comes to being judged about the job we are doing. Not, Mom or Dad, not friends or neighbors, God is our judge and He will judge our efforts according to His Word, His standard for excellence. If God will use His Word to judge us, then we must learn to do the Word to avoid that judgment. It is just like an open book test. We have the book, we know how we will be graded, the book we are reading not only has the questions, but the answers are there too. Once again, it's very simple, very precise, and very practical. God's system always works.

Revelation 3:19 NLT Jesus tells the church, *I correct and discipline everyone I love. So be diligent and turn from your indifference.*

The **Living Bible** adds, *become enthusiastic about the things of God.* Your marriage is a thing of God. The encouragement to turn from indifference, or replace passivity with passion applies to us men in our marriages today also. Most of us guys are diligent about going to work every day... with a weekly reward of a nice paycheck. We see that paycheck every week and it keeps us coming back for more.

Marital bliss should be the same way. We should reap the rewards for our diligence towards our spouses every day! The rewards should be smiles on each other's face, harmonious living, peaceful homes, agreement and power in our relationship. It's not just an ideal, it can become reality for us today. But it takes diligence!

James 1:22-25 NLT *But don't just listen to God's word. You must do what it says. Otherwise, you are only fooling yourselves. For, if you listen to the word and don't obey, it is like glancing at your face in a mirror. You see yourself, walk away, and forget what you look like. But if you look carefully into the perfect law that sets you free, and if you do what it says and don't forget what you heard, then God will bless you for doing it.*

You want to be blessed in your marriage. You want to be all that God has called you to be. You want to be blessed for doing it; then you have to take action and do what the Word of God says and not just listen and let it go in one ear and out the other.

All of the tasks of a husband which we have referred to in this book – that of a Governor, a Guard, and a Guide; and all of the roles, that of the Provider, the Peacemaker, the Ever Present Help, the Shepherd, and the Banner over your wife and home etc. are part of your marital duty. You have no excuse for not doing it because in God's kingdom, God has anointed the husband to do His job and to do it well. Notice that it is HIS JOB and not the man's own job according to his own criteria.

1 John 2:27 KJV *But the anointing which ye have received of him abideth in you,*

The anointing which you have received is not from Him, but it is of Him, and it lives in you to be able to accomplish this task.

In other words, God has placed a piece of Jesus in you. In your case husbands, you have received a piece of the Shepherd to guard your homes; you have received a piece of the Intercessor to pray for your family and to guide your home. You have received a piece of the Servant King to lay down your life for your wife and children daily in service and as Head of your family you have received a piece of the High Priest to stand present before God for your family's sake.

In short, you have a piece of the master inside you to help you to be diligent in ALL your marital responsibilities.

GOD has made YOU His very own
MASTER PIECE

TIME TO TALK

Proverbs 12 paints a great picture, your diligence can be a labor of love or just plain labor. Take inventory of your own efforts and identify the specific areas where you are laboring. Talk about them and see if you can initiate some action to turn your labor into a loving effort.

D = Diligent

The job we are doing as far as our marriages should not cause us shame. Talk about some areas in your marriage where you know your efforts are approved by God and perhaps those areas that not being approved by God, yet.

You will hear this time and time again, but it is so important. It is God who is working in you to do this stuff. He has anointed you, He has called you, He has gifted you with the ability to succeed in your marriage. Why do you think we continue to struggle then as husbands? What can we do about it to turn it around?

We will not only hear about how God has equipped us to be successful as husbands by the things he has placed in us, but can we think about and perhaps discuss our greatest helper on the earth today, besides the Holy Spirit, our wife. How is your wife helping you achieve your goal as a Godly husband? Name some specific areas were she excels.

Part Three

Chapter 9

THE ROLE OF THE WIFE

As with the husband in marriage, God has special assignments for the wives. Don't forget, the goal is to become one. God calls the man to a task of showing his wife what God looks like, and He calls the wife to a man. It's a divine calling, with special powers and abilities which enable the wife to help her husband in the marriage. Jesus paints the picture for the husband in marriage, while the Holy Spirit paints the picture for the wife in marriage.

The wife is not secondary in nature or ability to her husband. However, she has been made quite different than the man. She has been specifically created for the man. Just because God has placed the husband in charge for the sake of order, does not diminish the importance of the wife. They are team mates called to accomplish the same goal – ONEness.

There will be many challenges and trials ahead, but God knew that. There will be many times when the husband and wife will clash, but He knew that too. The idea is to stay the course and recognize that our differences are designed to enhance our ability to become one. Let's look at the specific gifts and callings God has given to the wife.

Genesis 2:18 NIV *And the LORD God said, "It is not good for the man to be alone; I will make a helper suitable to him."* ***v. 22*** *...and He brought her to the man.*

So we see that right off the bat, God never intended for man to be alone. He knew and still knows that we men need help. As we stay focused and remember that the goal is ONEness, we can see how God attempts to do this with two very different individuals.

Everything that He has told the husband to do for the wife is partly because He has created a similar need in her. The same goes for wives. God states that man should not be alone. It is not good for him to be alone. Well then, if it is not good for man to be alone, then the partner He created for the man will be gifted in the area of companionship for the man.

And it is not just a generic gift of companionship. It is a very specific gift. It is one woman, made for one man… for a lifetime. I like the word "suitable" because I think it's more descriptive and paints a better picture of the individuality of each marriage.

God brought Diane to me. She is not only made in the image of God, just like I am, but she has also been specifically suited to me. She is the only woman on the planet that has been technically, emotionally, spiritually, physically and intellectually sculpted to me. That is what suitable implies. I wear my wife like a fine fitting suit; she is warm and comfortable and makes me look better. But there is so much more. More often, when men purchase a suit, alterations are not only necessary, but they come as part of the deal of buying that suit. God loves Diane. He made her to be a certain way. You could say she has been tailor made; but now comes the alterations so that she fits me like the finest suit I could ever imagine. Hand crafted by the Master Himself.

The basic assignment that God gives to the wife is that of being a helper to her husband. We said it earlier, God calls the husband to a task of showing his wife what God looks like, but He calls the wife to a man. We will see though Scripture that her place of power is not in exalting herself or in self-promotion or self-gratification, but her place of power is when she makes her man look good. She does this through service, that of being a helper, and through submission, fitting into her husband's plans.

MARRIAGE MAINTENANCE TRUTH
Men Attain Greatness Through Accomplishment And Victory; Wives Attain Greatness Through Service And Submission

Not to worry ladies, this is not something you can't do. It is something you can do quite well and it is something you can do joyfully, because in the end it is what brings you your greatest fulfillment. Ultimately, you were specifically designed for such a purpose. You will see how you use your helpmate role to bring honor to the marriage. You will see how God has given you power to alter the course of mankind. You will come to learn that the term helpmate is an exalted position and not one of secondary citizenship in the Kingdom of God. Get ready, you are about to see God in a brand new and exciting and powerful way. You are about to see Him... in you!

The only other time we see the term "helper" used, in the same manner as when God applies it to the wife, is when God sends the Church a helper, the Holy Spirit.

John 16:7 NKJV *Nevertheless I tell you the truth. It is to your advantage that I go away; for if I do not go away, the Helper will not come to you; but if I depart, I will send Him to you.*

I don't think anyone would belittle the necessity of the existence or the power associated with the Holy Spirit. And yet, the very same word is used to describe both the wife and the Holy Spirit. God sent the Holy Spirit to the Church and God brought the wife to the man. Recognize that the Church needs a helper from God and that man also needs a helper from God. Both are needed in order for them to accomplish their assignments.

There are more similarities between the two. The Holy Spirit produces children for the Kingdom of God. Well, wives produce children in the marriage.

Romans 8:15 KJV The Holy Spirit is referred to as the *"Spirit of adoption, whereby we cry Abba; Father."*

Wives have a unique relationship with God's Holy Spirit throughout history. The prominent example of that relationship was when the angel came and spoke to Mary. He told Mary that she was highly favored and God's Holy Spirit would come upon her and the Messiah would be born through that union.

What a wonderful, powerful picture of what happens when a wife yields to the Holy Spirit. In this case, salvation was able to come through her for all mankind. Just apply that to a marriage, a wife yielding to the power of the Holy Spirit. The result will be no different; salvation is able to come to her husband and to her children.

Ladies, you can have the marriage you always dreamed about. You can have the man you believed he was on your wedding day as your life-long partner in marriage. Your challenge is the same as it was for Mary.

Luke 1:37-38 KJV *For with God nothing shall be impossible. And Mary said, Behold the handmaid of the Lord; be it unto me according to thy word. And the angel departed from her.*

Here it is ladies, it's all laid out for you right here. God's representative saying to Mary and to you too, *"For with God, nothing shall be impossible."* Then, Mary's heart revealed… *"be it unto me according to thy Word."* That's what it will take to see salvation for your husband and children. It will take a never ending confidence that if you believe, then absolutely *nothing will be impossible.* Then, if you truly will believe that, you will be able to say as Mary did… *be it unto me according to thy Word.*

You will need to know God's Word and let that Word rule and reign in your heart. We are very much aware of the battles wives are facing in marriages where the husbands are not on board as Christians. That's okay, to everything there is a season. What I wish to say to you as you read this book is that your season can be now.

Acts 16:31 NKJV … *"Believe on the Lord Jesus Christ, and you will be saved, you and your household."*

2 Peter 3:9 NKJV *God is not willing that any should perish but that all should come to repentance.*

God can make your marriage brand new. He can make your husband brand new too. Let's read on and begin releasing the power that has laid dormant in your lives and watch as God truly does begin to make your marriage ONEderful too!

TIME TO TALK

Ladies, how does the term "helper" make you feel? Does the fact the Holy Spirit has been assigned to the Church in the same manner a wife has been assigned to her husband give you a new depth of understanding towards your role? Can you talk about how you help your husband?

How are you able to manifest the companionship aspect of your relationship with your husband? Describe some of the obstacles you need to overcome to build this type of relationship.

Don't you just love the picture of Mary when she says to God's representative *"be it unto me according to thy word"?* What will it take on your part to be able to say the same thing? What are some of the changes you will have to make to achieve that goal?

Chapter 10

The Role of Respect

As wives learn to obey God, they will need to be fully persuaded that what they are doing is the will of God for their life. They will need to be committed to this task in the face of actions by their husband, for better or for worse, that may make this appear harder than it is. They may be discouraged by their husband's behavior that seems to make these efforts seem fruitless. It will be paramount ladies that you always have the picture of your husband before you found in the Word of God. That is what we did in the first half of this book. It will be what keeps you faithful and true in this assignment to your husbands.

The number one place in the Bible to see clearly what the role of the wife is in their marriage and how God expects them to act towards their husbands is in **Ephesians 5:33**, especially in the **Amplified Bible.** So for those of you that do not have an Amplified Bible handy, this is what is says.

> **Ephesians 5:33** *let the wife see that she respects and reverences her husband, that she notices him, regards him, honors him, prefers him, venerates and esteems him; and that she defers to him, praises him, and loves and admires him EXCEEDINGLY.*

I don't know about you, but when I hear the word exceedingly I immediately remember the Scripture in **Ephesians 3:20 KJV,** *Now unto HIM that is able to do exceeding abundantly above all that we ask or think, according to the power that worketh in us.*

There is a power in us wives to be able to do these things for our husbands. Therefore, ask yourself, are you loving your husband and admiring your husband above all that he could ask for or even think about? Are you going so overboard with your praise of him and for him, that he is asking you to stop because it's embarrassing him? As a husband, I would say, "TRY ME."

As a wife, you are supposed to be your husband's biggest cheerleader. Cheerleaders just don't cheer when the team is winning. They cheer the loudest when the team is down and needs some encouragement. Cheerleaders don't scream and yell out criticisms when the team is doing something wrong. Cheerleaders don't point out all their team's failures and show how disappointed they are in their team's performance. Cheerleaders may be kicking and screaming, but they are not supposed to kick and scream at their own team. Even at the end of the game, knowing the team has lost, they encourage those players with words of praise for what will happen the next time they play a game. Cheerleaders paint the picture of VICTORY always for their team. If there is going to be any discipline or correcting going on, it will come from the coach, or in our case, from God, not the cheerleader nor us wives.

I don't want to gloss over what **Ephesians 5:33 AMP** is trying to say, assuming that you have the full impact of each and every thing listed. Therefore, I will list the dictionary definitions of each one in order for you to fully comprehend the scope and depth of that Scripture.

As you go over them, individually, make a check list for yourself and see if you are living up to God's commands, or are you falling short in one aspect or another. Are you needing to work on a few and try harder on others? Here goes:

The Role of Respect

Respect - appreciation of worth and value

Reverence - profound respect mingled with awe and affection

Notice - pay attention and be aware of by commenting on or acknowledging

Regard - to look or think about in a certain specific way

Honor - an outward, visible token or act of respect

Prefer - to give priority to

Venerates - we judge to be of great worth and treat accordingly

Esteems - value greatly

Defers - to yield to the opinion or decision of

Praises - an expression of approval or commendation

Loves - a deep devotion or affection for or a strong passion for

Admires - to regard with wonder and pleasure

When we are trying to make a point, trying to make sure something we are saying to someone is hitting home, we repeat it. God realizes that respect and honor for a husband is not only necessary, but so vital in a marriage. Respect and honor is more than just being polite to someone, saying "Yes sir, or No ma'am." It is not just saying "Please and Thank you." God knows that respect and honor are crucial to a marriage, not only surviving but thriving, that He repeats what He said in **Ephesians**. He changes it up a little, He brings in a little more clarity, and He expects us to not only get the point, but to do it.

1 Peter 3:1 LB *Wives, fit in with your husbands plans, for then if they refuse to listen when you talk to them about the Lord, they will be won by your respectful,* *pure behavior. Your godly lives WILL SPEAK to them better than any words.*

1 Peter 3:2 AMP *When they [your husband] OBSERVE the pure and modest way in which you conduct yourselves, together with your reverence for your husband; you are to feel for him all that reverence includes: to respect, defer to, revere him, to honor, esteem, appreciate, prize, and in the human sense, to adore him, that is, to admire, praise, be devoted to, deeply love, and enjoy your husband.*

Again, we will look at the dictionary's definitions, and really hone in on what God is trying to teach us through His word.

Appreciate - to be fully aware of the value, importance and magnitude of and to show gratitude for

Prize - a reward for superiority or success, to value highly

Adore - to love and honor with intense devotion

Devoted - to apply attention, time, or oneself completely to

Deeply love - a learned or penetrating or intense feeling of

Enjoy - to take pleasure or joy in

Ladies, go through your check list again. Do you think we have some work to do? What would be your husbands' response?

MARRIAGE MAINTENANCE TRUTH
Wives Need To Honor Their Husband Based On Position And Not Performance.

Chapter 11

A Godly Wife is Wise

John 14:26 NKJV *But the Helper, the Holy Spirit, whom the Father will send in My name, He will teach you all things, and bring to your remembrance all things that I said to you.*

Ladies, in order for you to do all the things that you are called by God to do for your husband and for your marriage you must allow the Holy Spirit to teach you and to bring to your remembrance God's Word. Just as the Holy Spirit overshadowed Mary and brought forth something Holy, so too do you need the Holy Spirit to overshadow you and bring out the Holy thing that God has placed inside of you. That Holy thing is God's Wisdom.

Men, your wives are wise women. There is no argument; it's not up for a vote. All our wives are wise... period. God has somehow, someway, in His divine providence just made them that way. I don't know why God made men stronger than women. I could hazard a guess, but I won't. In the same manner, He has put wisdom in wives. I have known for years my wife is wise. I didn't say she is smarter than me, I just acknowledge that she is a wise wife.

Proverbs is full of Scriptures that talk about wisdom and just about every time, wisdom is referred to as a "she or her."

Proverbs 3:14 NLT *For wisdom is more profitable than silver, and her wages are better than gold.*

Proverbs 3:18 NLT *Wisdom is a tree of life to those who embrace her; happy are those who hold her tightly.*

Proverbs 4:8 AMP *Prize Wisdom highly and exalt her, and she will exalt and promote you; she will bring you to honor when you embrace her.*

Proverbs 1:20 NLT *Wisdom shouts in the streets. She cries out in the public square.*

Proverbs 8:1 NLT *Listen as Wisdom calls out! Hear as understanding raises her voice!*

Notice that last one? Wisdom has a voice. In my house it sounds a lot like my wife, Diane.

Proverbs 31:26 NLT *When she speaks, her words are wise, and she gives instructions with kindness.*

I thank God that when that wisdom speaks in my house, it comes in the presentation of a Kind Instructor. That's part of the wisdom package, wisdom knows how to get the most out of us men. Wisdom speaks to us honorably, never rude, never in a tone that is demeaning. There is a way that we will hear our wives instruction and the wise wife knows how to deliver it… kindly. No getting around it guys, our wives are wise women. They not only are wise women, but they crave wisdom too.

<u>**Genesis 3:6**</u> **NLT** *The woman was convinced. She saw that the tree was beautiful and its fruit looked delicious, and she wanted the wisdom it would give her.*

A Godly Wife is Wise

Look at the Scripture in Genesis. What is it Eve desired? Eve desired the apple, yes, but why? Because she wanted the wisdom that it would give her. If the enemy had gotten to Adam first the apple might have been power, but he went to Eve and the apple that he dangled was wisdom. I guess that desire for wisdom is inherent in them. Look at the Queen of Sheba when she heard how God had blessed Solomon with wisdom.

1 Kings 10:6-9 MSG *She said to the king, "It's all true! Your reputation for accomplishment and wisdom that reached all the way to my country is confirmed. I wouldn't have believed it if I hadn't seen it for myself; they didn't exaggerate! Such wisdom and elegance—far more than I could ever have imagined.*

The Queen of Sheba traveled many miles to see the wisdom of Solomon for herself, and she was not disappointed. Neither will you, husbands, if you go looking for the wisdom God has placed in your wife.

Christian wives are especially wise women. In addition to the wisdom they have just because they are our wives, they add to that, the wisdom of the Word. There are not too many things that are wiser than a wife who studies the Word of God and then follows through by living out what she has learned. It takes a husband and a wife and their God to build the kind of home, and create the kind of spiritual atmosphere where they can raise their children, and walk in the promise of salvation for their entire household. It not only takes a husband and a wife and their God, but it takes a special woman.

Proverbs 14:1 NLT *A wise woman builds her home, but a foolish woman tears it down with her own hands.*

It takes a wise woman to build her home. I believe that the covenant of marriage does something to a woman that automatically engages a supernatural ability for them to walk in wisdom. Just like the institution of marriage is holy and certain things take place as soon as a man and a woman enter into that covenant, so too does it seem like a "wisdom gene" all of a sudden kicks in to the wife. It may have to do with the "grace of life" that is only offered to a husband and a wife as **1 Peter 3:7 KJV** says. There is such wisdom evident in wives today, especially those that follow hard after God's Word.

> **Proverbs 14:1 MSG** *Lady Wisdom builds a lovely home.*

I just love the phrase "Lady Wisdom." Notice it is "Lady" in front of wisdom. The implication is clear; wisdom in itself is gracious and kind. You could very easily say, wisdom is lady like. Wisdom follows all the rules that God has set out for it. Wisdom isn't rude or unruly, but rather wisdom follows the plan from God to reveal herself to us and in us. I can tell when Diane is operating in God's wisdom just by the way she speaks to me. There is no demand, no heavy handed verbal manipulation; it's just a peaceable request, or a gentle suggestion.

> **James 3:17 NLT** *But the wisdom from above is first of all pure. It is also peace loving, gentle at all times, and willing to yield to others. It is full of mercy and good deeds. It shows no favoritism and is always sincere.*

My wife wears wisdom quite well thank you. That wisdom, when it is delivered like that doesn't threaten me at all. She is called to be my helpmate and I recognize that as such. I receive the wisdom that she offers and the end result is that I have made the correct decision, or I have grown in an area where I needed to. Once again, it is God's perfect plan coming to fruition.

Do I believe that in marriage perhaps God withholds certain things from me as a husband so that He can place them in Diane? Absolutely! If we are to become one then we need to offer one another gifts that appeal to one another. We need to come into this relationship with what God has given each of us for the other. Then, we need to present these gifts, this wisdom, at the proper time and place where it will be received. This is all part of the ONEness process.

I am not saying God made us husbands dumb so that our wives could be wise. I am saying that God has also made us husbands wise. We are wise enough to walk in humility when we know we need help. Then we are wise enough to know that there is a very good chance that the thing we may need is the personal helpmate that He designed specifically for us. I like that a lot!

Proverbs 31:26 NKJV *She opens her mouth with wisdom, And on her tongue is the law of kindness.*

Most of us husbands didn't need a Scripture to tell us that. We already know it as fact. Here, it is revealed as truth. It doesn't say maybe she does, or perhaps she does, no, the Scripture plainly states that the **Proverbs 31** woman *opens her mouth with wisdom*. Receive this as truth guys and live happily ever after and in harmony with one another.

Titus 2:4 AMP *So that they [older women] will wisely train the young women to be sane and sober of mind (temperate, disciplined) and to love their husbands and their children,*

Wives are not only wise in dealing with their husbands; they are very wise in other areas too! This wisdom will extend to all her relationships. Everything a wife does should be done with the wisdom God has instilled in her. It is one of her greatest gifts and the Godly wife should just flow in this area.

Proverbs 1:20 MSG *Lady Wisdom goes out in the street and shouts. At the town center she makes her speech.*

This wisdom that God has placed in wives should be evident to all. Everyone that I know understands that my wife is a wise woman. It should be that way in your homes too. Remember ladies, **Proverbs 18:16 NKJV** says that *a person's gift will make room for them.* Your wisdom should open doors for you in the appointed area of your ministry. Expect to see God in a greater way as you flow in this wisdom in your marriage. Know that this gifting is not to make you look good, but it is for God's glory and He receives glory when you use His wisdom… to make your husband look good.

A wise woman will always vision her husband for greatness. A part of that beginning story for Joel & Victoria Osteen becoming the Pastors of Lakewood Church was the TV program itself that Pastor Joel's dad had all over the world. With all the commitments and schedules for programming that Pastor John had, who would want to hear what Joel had to say now that Pastor John was gone. So Joel cancelled all the contracts.

When he got home and told Victoria, she encouraged him to keep those contracts and all those commitments. They were for prime time slots on prime stations. She convinced him that people would want to hear what God had placed on the inside of him, just as she had enjoyed hearing him for all these years. It was the weekend and nothing could be done about reversing the cancellations until Monday. She had confidence though that all would be well until then, and she was right. Every one he had called on Friday, decided not to do anything about rescheduling those time slots until Monday. So they were still there, ready for Joel to pick them back up.

Where would Joel be now if it had not been for the wisdom God had placed in Victoria for such a time as that?

TIME TO TALK

The wisdom that God has placed in wives has many facets to it. Wives are also very wise concerning their children. Often they know when something is wrong or when the children might be less than truthful. This wisdom comes with knowledge, understanding and discernment. Give a recent example where you felt you demonstrated that wisdom.

Proverbs 3:14 NLT says that *"For wisdom is more profitable than silver, and her wages are better than gold."* How would you say wisdom has profited you?

It's interesting that the phrase "homemaker" is applied to wives. **Proverbs 14:1 MSG** says, *"Lady Wisdom builds a lovely home."* Part of the wife's ministry to her family is to turn a house into a home. Of course it's a process and doesn't happen overnight. What are some of the things that you have contributed towards that goal?

Whether it seems like it or not, your husband is created by God to hear your wisdom. He may not listen at times, but he does hear you. Take stock of your situation and see if you have been presenting that wisdom as it should be according to **James 3:17 NLT.** What suggestions might you make to other wives that would help them speak into their husband's lives?

Chapter 12

How Wives **INFLUENCE** their Husbands

John 16:13 KJV *Howbeit when He, the Spirit of truth, is come, He will guide you into all truth: for He shall not speak of himself; but whatsoever He shall hear, that shall He speak: and He will shew you things to come.*

Wives have the exact same assignment. They are to influence their husbands by guiding them to the truth; the truth as seen through God's word and not necessarily her own.

Man is called by God to be the main breadwinner in the family and he is also called by God to Govern, Guard and Guide the home. The wife is called by God to Guide her husband also through the investment of the Word. Together they become a team looking out for the welfare of the family. A wife accomplishes this task by being sensitive to the Holy Spirit.

Since the time of Mary giving birth to Christ, women have always had a sensitive connection to God's Spirit, more so than man. The bond that was created then still exists today. Women need to tap into that sensitivity in order to fulfill their calling.

In the most negative sense of a wife influencing her husband, we see how a flesh driven Eve, influenced Adam. Her assignment was to remind Adam what God had said, but she didn't. At a time when Eve should have been influencing Adam with… "Thus saith the Lord" or even… "Has God not said"? Eve was tricked into allowing her husband to sin. The result was catastrophic. Can you imagine what would have happened if Eve had done her job? The point is ladies... look at the power that is available to you as you fulfill your assignment in influencing your husband.

My wife Diane and I, attend Lakewood Church in Houston, Texas. Joel and Victoria Osteen are our Pastors. Victoria has said many times to the ladies of the church... "be careful of what you speak to your husbands, because the words you say to him have the ability to change his heart." That is so wise and so true. If God has placed the wife in the home to remind her husband what the Holy Spirit is saying, then He has placed within the husband the ability to hear his wife. Use that knowledge to the benefit of the marriage and make sure your words are encouraging words, life giving words that will set in motion thoughts that will highlight his dreams.

Let's use another example of the way a wife can influence her husband. Let's bring it into today's world, let's bring it right into our own home. Ladies, you must know that most men are turned on sexually by what they see. Women have been influencing men visually for as long as we have been around. It's been said men need pictures and in this sense it is absolutely correct. Well, let's look at a powerful Scripture that will show you how to use this knowledge for God's good.

> **1 Peter 3:1-2 NLT** *In the same way, you wives must accept the authority of your husbands. Then, even if some refuse to obey the Good News, your godly lives will speak to them without any words. They will be won over by observing your pure and reverent lives*

This is one of the most powerful Scriptures in the Bible for you wives. You need to read this Scripture everyday and make it a part of who you are. If you can turn your husband on sexually by what he sees, then you can also turn your husband on spiritually by what he sees.

God says that your husbands *will be won over by OBSERVING your pure and reverent life.* **The New King James version** says it this way... *when they observe your chaste conduct accompanied by fear.* That's right, WHEN they observe.

God promises you wives that if you will do certain things, He promises that your husband will notice. He not only promises that your husband will notice, He promises that when he notices, it will produce the desired result.

Look at that, you can influence your husband by living a Godly life. Men are visual, men need pictures, c'mon gals, let's use that knowledge and bring your husband into the godly place he needs to be. Influence your husband by living a Godly life.

The importance of this Scripture is so crucial in a wife's ability to be used by God to help bring her husband to the place God wants him to be, that we will use this Scripture over and over and over again in many different translations to make our point. Layer upon layer of wisdom from God, will be revealed to wives for their husband and their marriage. What a great gift from God.

1 Peter 3:1-2 NKJV *Wives, likewise, be submissive to your own husbands, that even if some do not obey the word, they, without a word, may be won by the conduct of their wives, when they observe your chaste conduct accompanied by fear*

God is speaking to wives here. He says... wives, be submissive to your own husbands. I know lots of women who struggle with that, and if the truth be known, they should. But they should struggle only if they are not saved. Women, rebelling against the authority of the man is part of the curse, but as Christians, *we have been redeemed from the curse of the law* **(Gal. 3:13 NKJV).**

God is telling the wives here to be submissive to their husbands EVEN IF SOME DO NOT OBEY THE WORD. Okay, God is talking to wives here who are married to non-believing husbands. God says, to obey them, submit to them, and honor them without a word. You can say that God is saying "Shut Up" to the wives. He goes on to say they may be won by the conduct of their wives.

One wise woman in our class said, "Sometimes you have to duck in order for God to get a clean shot." In other words, "Get out of the way, and let God." Remember that redemption, being saved, being born again is God's plan for you and your husband and your family. Don't you think that the Creator of the Plan would know best how to implement it; how to bring it to pass?

That Scripture is so powerful. Look, God says basically, wives, be quiet and let your godly lifestyle do the talking. But He promises you something when you do that. He promises that they "MAY" be won. That's not a "may" as in maybe or perhaps, that is a "may" as in granting permission. Do you see it? God says that when you wives are quiet and get out of the way and live a holy, godly life, you have just GRANTED GOD PERMISSION to win your husbands. Basically, you are using your lives to influence your husband instead of your mouth. What's that saying? Don't spend so much time talking to your husband about God, but spend that time talking to God about your husband!

God says when you do that; I WILL cause your husband to observe your behavior. Ladies, use your power of influence in the realm of the Spirit. Live holy lives in your home and let God do the rest. Everything you need to get past the submission problem, everything you need to win your husband is right in there. Just remember, God has equipped you greatly to influence your husband.

MARRIAGE MAINTENANCE TRUTH
Husbands Are Created By God With The Distinct Ability To Be Influenced By Their Wives

Let me clarify one point here, we are never saying to the wives, you must submit to your husband even if he asks you to do something illegal or ungodly. **NO, NO, NO!!!!**

But there is a way to respectfully tell him NO, and not usurp his authority as a husband or as the head of home. That way is to get the third party of your marriage covenant directly involved through intercession and prayer. God has a responsibility, not only to each of you but to the marriage as well. You invited Him into the marriage in the first place, didn't you?

> **1 Corinthians 11:3 NKJV** *But I want you to know that the head of every man is Christ, the head of woman is man, and the head of Christ is God.*

Christ is the head of the husband, whether the husband will admit that or not. Therefore, I can go to my husband's head and ask Him to influence my husband to make the correct decision or do the right thing as He sees fit.

TIME TO TALK

Ladies have been influencing men since the beginning of time. It is almost the "default" position in a marriage relationship. Looking back on your lives ladies, recall the times when you have influenced your husband, either intentionally or not. Will you acknowledge that God has made you with that ability? Looking ahead now, in what area would you most like to see your influence used?

After reading this chapter, do you think you will have a greater sensitivity about using your influence? In what way?

Your influence over your husband is actually a powerful spiritual force that is to be used to help God help him. It's a special gift from God that insures your husband's success in all areas. Identify areas where your husband may be struggling with success and then ask God how you can be used to help him through your gifting of influence. Verbalize your commitment to your husband.

Has there ever been an instance where you asked God to influence your husband when you thought that your husband was making the wrong decision. What was your attitude toward your husband before God intervened? What was your husband's response to you when he realized you saved him from making a mistake?

Chapter 13

How Wives **INSPIRE** Their Husbands

Since we just finished the chapter on "How wives INFLUENCE their husbands", the most important difference between influence and inspire is this: Influence is pressure given to something from the outside, while Inspire is from within.

I don't know about the rest of you guys, but I married my biggest cheerleader. Truth be told, she probably was my only cheerleader too. But my wife is an expert at cheering me on. And we guys have a long history of needing that aspect of encouragement in our lives. We need to be encouraged. We see it every day at all sorts of sporting events. We see women on the sidelines, cheering on their teams. It's no different in marriage. Wives are to be their husband's biggest cheerleaders.

Diane is always in my corner. She inspires me in many ways but she is especially skilled at lifting me up verbally and telling me how anointed I am. She encouraged me to write this book, or create that lesson, or go sell that job. She has never put down my abilities (or lack there of). I don't even know if she is aware of my limitations. She speaks to those things that God has implanted within me, and inspires me to "Go for the Gold." This steadfast faith in me inspires me and dares me to be better. That's one of the best things I like about my wife. She is easily fooled. No, just kidding, she is unwavering in her support for me.

Another way my wife inspires me is that she always does things with excellence. I am just a noisy, clanging Sanguine temperament. She is a perfectionist melancholy. Her standard is usually so much higher than mine. Because I know that she loves me and is in my corner, I don't feel threatened by this, but rather I am inspired by her to be better, to stretch toward my full potential.

Once again, my Pastors, Joel and Victoria Osteen, are great examples of how a wife can inspire her husband. Two such dramatic examples come immediately to my mind.

When Pastor John Osteen went home to be with the Lord, no one was quite sure who the mantle of leadership was going to fall on to pastor Lakewood Church. For years and years prior to this event, Victoria would tell Joel that he was going to pastor Lakewood someday. No way! He was totally content being in the background, taking care of his parents and their world wide TV program. Joel preach?! What a ridiculous idea that was. Yet that prophetic word that had been planted by Victoria for all those years rose up in due season and the rest is history as they say.

When Lakewood Church was being relocated to our current campus, Pastor Joel would tell the story about the opposition he was facing in acquiring our current facility. The potential was there for him to be discouraged, but he tells how his wife, Victoria, kept cheering him on. He speaks with great respect that she would not let the dream die. She kept on planting seeds in him, that it was all going to work out for the better. And of course, it did. Pastor Joel acknowledges what a huge part Victoria played in continually lifting him up and filling him with hope and inspiring him with her words that it was going to be okay. Again, the rest is history.

There is a time and a place to speak to your husband and to inspire him with your words; to be that cheerleader rooting him on.

Proverbs 10:21 NLT *The words of the godly encourage many,*

My personal Love Language is Words of Affirmation. Lots of men have that as their primary Love Language also. I am inspired to do better when people encourage me with their words. I tell couples in our class all the time, if you want a friend for life, just tell me how good I did. That encourages and inspires me to keep giving you my best. This is exactly what great women do for their men. Victoria does it for Pastor Joel and my wife does it for me. Here's one more Scripture so that you wives can see the power in inspiring your husband verbally by filling them with Words of Affirmation.

Proverbs 10:11 NLT *The words of the godly are a life-giving fountain;*

Words from a life-giving fountain is something to be taken inside of you; words that will inspire you and motivate you from within. What beverage were you serving your husband last week? We husbands need that life-giving beverage and we need it from our wives the most. Would you really want that beverage being served to your husband by someone else? Whether this is currently evident in your marriage or not, husbands are called by God to hear their wives. Your words ladies are to be going down deep inside your husband and bringing life to his dreams, helping him to reach his destiny.

Proverbs 25:11 NKJV *A word fitly spoken is like apples of gold in settings of silver.*

This is one of my favorite Scriptures in the Bible. When you break it down it just reeks of inspiration. I heard a Pastor's wife speak on this and it just went off in my heart.

She broke it down, checked out the words in the Hebrew and when it was all said and done it came out something like this... your words are to set in motion the illumination of the imaginations of the mind... or as I like to phrase it, your words are to remind someone of their dreams. What a great description of inspiration.

Ladies, you have the ability, no you have the responsibility, to keep your husband's dreams before him. Don't let them die! No one else will support him and lift him up like you can. If he is struggling, then it becomes your finest hour. Remind him of what he always wanted to become. Point out his goodness and his strengths. Let him know you will help him quench the very fires of hell that have come against him, if that's what it takes. He has got to know that you are in this for the long haul and even though things may not look good now, God has placed you together and you are going to make it. Challenge him to be his very best by letting him see your very best as you inspire him.

Proverbs 10:32 NLT *The lips of the godly speak helpful words,*

Helpmates should be speaking helpful words. Allow God to mold you into the helper, representing His Holy Spirit to your husband, through the words you speak. God knows us men need help. I need help from my wife to keep me inspired to pursue my dreams for our life. When I know and hear that my baby is on my side I can move mountains. I can grow that much quicker. I feel like I can leap tall buildings in a single bound! Why, I can even write a book!

In the last chapter, we briefly touched on how to influence your husband by being submissive to them. We will take a closer look back at that Scripture and see how being submissive to them will inspire them also.

1 Peter 3:1-2 NKJV *Wives, likewise, be submissive to your own husbands, that even if some do not obey the word, they, without a word, may be won by the conduct of their wives, when they observe your chaste conduct accompanied by fear.*

Wives must be submissive to their own husband. In this Scripture, the husband is not obeying the Word of God, and therefore, the husband is not submitting to the will of God. Wives have a great opportunity here to inspire their husbands to do that by her actions. The Scripture doesn't say she does it verbally. Agreeing to do something but grumbling on the inside is not truly being submissive.

The Scripture doesn't say they are to pray about it. No, the Scripture here says that the husband will be won by the conduct of their wife being submissive along with her actions. Remember, men are visual. Wives need to paint the picture of being submissive. Husbands need to see the attitude of her heart as she is being submissive to him. It is the thing that is within her that will speak to his heart within him. How does that happen? Wives show husbands what submission is, not by submitting to God, that's not what the Scripture says. They do this by submitting to THEIR HUSBAND.

Watch what happens. When men see wives submitting to God they say, ho hum, that's nice. But when wives begin to submit to their husband it is a whole new ballgame. Men are no longer merely observers, but they have been brought into the submission process. They are no longer just looking at a picture of submission, but they have now become the canvas upon which the picture of submission is being painted. By submitting to their husbands, the wives have brought their husbands into actually experiencing submission as God experiences submission. They now understand submission not by seeing it but by living it. When wives treat their husband like they treat God, husbands can experience the presence of God whether they are seeking Him or not.

MARRIAGE MAINTENANCE TRUTH
Submission In Marriage Is The Wife's Place Of Power

MARRIAGE MAINTENACE TRUTH
Inspiration Through Submission Gives Husbands The Honor They Crave

Understand it or not ladies, you have brought your husband into the presence of God. It's what women have been trying to do for centuries, but they have been trying to do it the wrong way. Ladies have been trying it their way, in their own knowledge. No, it must be done God's way for true success. We apply His principles, we are motivated by His love in us for our husband and we are directed by the Holy Spirit, not our flesh, and it WILL WORK every time. You have God's Word, God's Promise on that.

> **Proverbs 3:5-6 NKJV** *Trust in the LORD with all your heart, And lean not on your own understanding; In all your ways acknowledge Him, And He shall direct your paths.*

TIME TO TALK

After hearing about the difference between "Influence" and "Inspiration" ladies, do you see the difference? Make a list of, or better yet, discuss with your husband how you might be inspiring him.

Look at the Scriptures that talk about how our words are to be encouraging each other. I love the one where it says, *our words are as a "life giving fountain."* Couple that with your calling to help your husband be all that he can be in Christ, and you should be able to see how necessary speech like that is to your husband. Lord knows we get beat up enough outside the home. What can you do to create an environment for him that will be one of encouragement and full of that *"life giving"* beverage?

Hopefully, ladies, you are seeing submission in a new light. You have such power available to you. Can you identify what changes you will make and would you be willing to share these with your husband?

Look at that list of things that a wife is to do for her husband in the beginning of this Chapter, from **1 Peter 3:2 AMP.** How can you increase those elements in your marriage? Going through that list, one by one, what can you start to ramp up immediately and which ones are going to become a continued work in progress for you?

Chapter 14

Four Tasks God Assigns To A *W. I. F. E.* As She Helps Her Husband

According to Proverbs 31 NLT we can see how a wife is to be a ***W**orker* to her family. She does this by ***I**nstructing* those in her care in the spirit of both wisdom and kindness. By becoming a ***F**riend*, she continues the process of ONEness with her husband. Through this godly, energetic lifestyle she becomes an ***E**xample* for her entire family, neighborhood, and community to follow.

*W = **W**orker*

In marriage, God has called the man to a task; that of loving his wife and showing his family what God looks like. We must understand that God also has a calling on the wife. Her calling is to a man, her husband. In order for the wife to fulfill her marital calling, she has been assigned duties or WORK within the marriage to insure her husband's and ultimately the marriage's success.

Proverbs 31:17 NLT *She is energetic and strong, a hard worker.*

The New International version – *She sets about her work vigorously; her arms are strong for her tasks.*

The Amplified version – *She girds herself with strength, spiritual, mental, and physical fitness for her God-given task and makes her arms strong and firm.*

The Message Bible version – *First thing in the morning, she dresses for work, rolls up her sleeves, eager to get started.* ***v.18*** *...she is in no hurry to call it quits for the day.*

The **Proverbs 31** wife is not only a strong and hard worker but she is eager to get started, totally engaged with her task, and delays stopping. She knows what demands the marriage makes upon her as a wife and mother and she runs to heed the call.

In the beginning of **Proverbs 31:18 MSG** it states an interesting truth, *"She senses the worth of her work."* When we, whether as a man or a woman begin to understand our role, our calling, our gifting, we should be able to sense the value or the worth in our efforts. This should lead to fulfillment in your life.

Wives should not be looking for other areas or for other activities to bring them this sense of fulfillment. Sensing the value in what God has called them to do in the marriage should satisfy their deepest needs and desires. That doesn't mean she is not involved with other projects, some perhaps even outside the home. It just means that her greatest anointing, the place where she can manifest the power and the presence of God most, will be in ministry to her family at home.

Proverbs 31:13 NKJV   *...And willingly works with her hands.*

The New International version – *...and works with eager hands.*

The New American Standard Bible – *...and works with her hands in delight.*

The Godly wife works how? Not begrudgingly, but she willingly works with her hands, eager to do it, and it gives her a sense of delight. This sounds a lot like the way we are to be *"cheerful givers"* (**2 Cor. 9:7 NKJV**). This is a sure sign that she is totally committed to God by her obedience to His Word and continues that commitment to her husband and the ministry of service to her family.

Titus 2:4-5 NLT *These older women must train the younger women to love their husbands and their children, to live wisely and be pure, to work in their homes, to do good, and to be submissive to their husbands. Then they will not bring shame on the word of God.*

God commands the more mature wives to train the younger wives as part of their work assignment. Train them how? Train them *to love their husband and children.* The older women must train the younger women to *be submissive to their husbands.* We talked about that in the previous chapters, but hopefully you can see how important this must be to God to keep bringing it up over and over again. So ladies, don't ignore this important truth. Also she trains them to *"work in their homes."*

Now, before you get all upset with me saying, "what about my job"? No where does it say wives can not work outside the home. As a matter of fact, the **Proverbs 31** wife is quite the entrepreneur with projects going on outside the home as well. We'll explore that aspect in a minute, but the

Word does insist that wives are to be workers in the home. *"Chaste, keepers at home,"* is how **The King James version** says it. **The Message version in verse 19** says, *She's skilled in the crafts of home and hearth, diligent in homemaking.* Sounds like an old-fashioned housewife to me.

I highlighted the last part of that Scripture in **Titus** because I did not want you to miss one of the most important elements of this Scripture. The "WHY" or reason your role as a Godly wife consists of all these responsibilities. You will *bring shame on the word of God* if you don't. That is an amazing point, but look at it in some of the other translations and the seriousness with which it states this truth.

The New International version – *so that no one will malign the word of God.*

The New American Standard Bible – *so that the word of God will not be dishonored.*

The Amplified version – *that the word of God may not be exposed to reproach blasphemed or discredited.*

Just so that you don't think God is being too hard on you wives, think about what the word says to husbands who don't fulfill their obligations and meet their families' responsibilities.

1 Timothy 5:8 KJV *But if any [husband] provide not for his own, and specially for those of his own house, he hath denied the faith, and is worse than an infidel.*

How would you like to be called an infidel every time you didn't make the bed or cook dinner or wash the dishes? So think about that the next time you want to start complaining about your responsibilities as a married woman. Just as God will anoint and strengthen the husband to do all that he is called by God to do, trust God to do the same for you. Work as unto the Lord, let that be your reasonable service to the Lord by offering the sacrifice of praise in the midst of your duties, and watch the rewards that will come from your obedience to God.

Proverbs 31:31 NLT *Reward her for all she has done. Let her deeds publicly declare her praise.*

The Message version – *Give her everything she deserves! Festoon her life with praises!*

I must admit that I did not know what *FESTOON* meant, so I looked it up in Webster's Dictionary. It talked about flowers and leaves, colored paper and ribbons, and to decorate. I thought of the word festival with all the hoopla that goes with it. I got the picture of what **The Message** Bible was saying, do you?

Now to the **Proverbs 31** wife as **an entrepreneur,** this wife can do it all.

Proverbs 31:16 AMP *She considers a new field before she buys or accepts it expanding prudently and not courting neglect of her present duties by assuming other duties; with her savings of time and strength she plants fruitful vines in her vineyard.*

Notice the Godly wife has the blessing from the Word to be industrious outside the scope of her household duties, but notice yet the admonishment, that she still must *"not neglect her present duties by assuming other duties."* See how this woman has created extra time and garnered extra funds for this extra endeavor by *"prudently"* managing both her time and money. The unsaid, yet implied meaning is clear here, regular work in the home comes first. That has priority over the extra work she assigns herself and it does not get left undone for her husband to do it.

Many women who work outside the home complain that their husbands do not help them around the house enough. This may sound old-fashioned, but according to the Word it never states that the husband is to be a *"keeper of the home."* I am not saying that husbands should not help around the house. Diane's Love Language is Acts of Service. I fill her love tank when I vacuum or clean the ceiling fan. But Diane is mindful not to make demands on me for the things she is responsible for in the home. She is careful not to make them my responsibility.

Let's look at what else this amazing woman and wife can do to earn extra income for her family. I will pull a few Scriptures from **Proverbs 31 NLT** and paint a picture of this very capable and virtuous entrepreneur.

v.13 - *She finds wool and flax and busily spins it.*

v.19 - *Her hands are busy spinning thread, her fingers twisting fiber.*

v.24 - *She makes belted linen garments and sashes to sell to the merchants.*

v.11 - *The heart of her husband trusts in her confidently and relies on and believes in her securely, so that he has no lack of honest gain or need of dishonest spoil.*

All I can say after that is WOW !!!!! What a woman. Yet the Word has a little more to say than just WOW !!!!!

Proverbs 31:28-31 NLT *Her children stand and bless her. Her husband praises her; "There are many virtuous and capable women in the world, but you surpass them all!" Charm is deceptive, and beauty does not last; but a woman who fears the LORD will be greatly praised. Reward her for all she has done. Let her deeds publicly declare her praise.*

She will be rewarded for her faithfulness. Her investment will not return void. It will produce Godly children and a loving husband. Her works will do the praising. No works... no praise.

TIME TO TALK

In your own life ladies, can you agree that you are able to "sense the worth" of the work you are doing for your husband and children? Does it give you that sense of fulfillment in your life? How is your husband able to know that? In what way does he recognize that you are centered on God's will in the home?

If you were to list the activities of your day, what would that list look like? What would be the first item on that list? Would it paint a picture of someone who is diligent at home or would it paint a picture of someone who is busy outside the home? Do you see that perhaps some adjustments may need to be made in order for you to come to the place where your own works can praise you?

She is the Selfless Servant

Jesus has called you to greatness ladies. He has given you the power to change the destiny of mankind as revealed in **Genesis** when Eve convinced Adam to take the apple. He has anointed you to win the hearts of your husbands through the way you live as pointed out in **1 Peter**. He has gifted you with the privilege of not only bearing new life in this earth, but also the responsibility of nurturing those new lives.

God trusts you. He trusts you with the newborn and He trusts you with us men. He trusts you to let the Holy Spirit live through you in a singular way that will reveal God's will to your husband. He trusts you by planting within you a special wisdom that is there and ready for your husband to use. He trusts you to show the power of His Holy Spirit and the greatness of Christ.

This greatness is best revealed when a woman gets married. It is the ultimate sacrifice, someone laying down their life for another.

John 15:13 NKJV *Greater love has no one than this, than to lay down one's life for his friends.*

Just by the inherent nature of marriage, this is what a woman does. She lays down her life. She willfully lays down the ability to make certain decisions. She gives up her plans of a career perhaps. She places her future in the hands of another. She voluntarily says she will give up her freedom, her individuality to serve another. That's "Greater Love." That's the greater love that John was talking about. It is the ultimate sacrifice. It is the mark of the servant. It is the absolute very finest picture of Christ that one could make. And the Godly wife makes that sacrifice, becomes that selfless servant, lays down her life… every day.

There should be no way a man can ever leave his home in the morning without being cognizant of the fact that his wife paints him the picture of Jesus' love every day. There is no way a man should ever think that his wife is not his friend. He sees this born out every day when he comes home and his wife is there; her commitment still binding, her love still holding her there. Truth be told, us men wouldn't do it, us men couldn't do it. If God told us we had to stay in the marriage and we would not be in charge, we would be gone. If God laid it out where all we had to do each day was build our lives around our wives, we'd be gone. If God told us we would serve them every day without reward or glory, we'd be gone.

That's right. God places within the wife the ability to willingly lay down her life in service to help us achieve greatness. Our greatness is in large part a manifestation of their greatness. Diane's gifts are for me, to make me look good. She has already said she would lay down her life to do this. Now it's on me to achieve the success or victory she is believing in me for.

When was the last time one of us men said we would sacrifice a golf game, a vacation with the boys, or a big ball game so that we could stay home and fit in with our wives' plans? When have we helped promote that plan and make it a success so that our wife's gifts and greatness would be recognized by others? If there is any one group in the world today who is without excuse for coming to the saving knowledge of the grace of God through Christ it would be a husband. We are faced with the service of Christ every minute of every day.

I can't remember the last time my wife complained about doing this either. Truth be told, if I am great, it is because she is great. Truth be told; in order for me to achieve this greatness, she must be great first. Me as a husband, achieving greatness without the service of my wife is a hindrance to the process of intimacy and has the potential to prevent the **one**ness that is marriage's goal.

You have to know this men, your wife becomes great on your wedding day. Yours may be in hiding, your potential sitting on go, but your greatness has not yet been revealed. But when she says "I do" she immediately enters into the arena of greatness and the ball has been put in play for the marriage to succeed.

> **Mark 10:43 NIV** *Not so with you. Instead, whoever wants to become great among you must be your servant,*

It is so evident, these truths about greatness in husbands and wives, and yet we tend to miss it. The world distracts us where we are not seeing things as God has laid them out. As often as you think about being a success guys, as often as you desire that big sale or that new job, as often as you think about being "promoted," that is as often as your wife is thinking about how to help you. God doesn't give a man "Dream A" and then give "Dream B" to the wife. He wants us on the same page.

Diane and I always say, we are not only reading from the same book, but we are on the same page. But this won't work if the husband is walking in the flesh and the wife is walking in the Spirit. Our dreams are created in the spirit and God has made us to find them in our spirit walk. Our wives' service is ultimately to make us successful in all areas, emotionally, spiritually, healthy physically and socially. Their job truly is a labor of love and they excel at it every day.

TIME TO TALK

Being a selfless servant fits the role of the wife so well. Can you ladies see how this role might give you an advantage over us men in building a relationship with Christ? In what way?

Jesus is the ultimate servant. He did what He did for us "while we were yet sinners." Does that "while we were yet sinners" phrase ever apply to your task also? Are you able to still be the selfless servant even when your husband isn't at his best? Have you ever seen the rewards for this? Talk about them.

God's place for your greatness is through service and submission. Does that threaten you at all? Are you okay with that? Why?

Chapter 15

W. *I*. F. E.

According to Proverbs 31 NLT we can see how a wife is to be a **Worker** to her family. She does this by **Instructing** those in her care in the spirit of both wisdom and kindness. By becoming a **Friend**, she continues the process of ONEness with her husband. Through this godly, energetic lifestyle she becomes an **Example** for her entire family, neighborhood, and community to follow.

I = *Instructor*
(a kind instructor)

John 14:26 NKJV *But the Helper, the Holy Spirit, whom the Father will send in My name, He will teach you all things, and bring to your remembrance all things that I said to you.*

Don't forget ladies, just as Jesus is the perfect example of how a husband is to *"love his wife **as** Christ loves the Church,"* so too is the Holy Spirit the perfect example of how a wife instructs her husband. By seeing how the Holy Spirit instructs the Church, she learns how to instruct her husband. Remember, the wife was given to the husband as a helper, just as the Holy Spirit was given to the Church as a HELPER also. Just as the Holy Spirit brings to remembrance God's Word to us, you are to bring to your husband's remembrance what God's Word has said too. The key point here is the way this wisdom, this instruction, is delivered.

Proverbs 31:26 NLT *When she speaks her words are wise, and she gives instructions with kindness.*

It's not just instruction that a wife is to give her husband and her family, but it's kind instruction. The reason it is delivered in this kindness mode is because she is never to usurp his authority or contradict him in front of others.

1 Timothy 2:12 KJV *But I suffer not a woman to teach, nor to usurp authority over the man,*

Usurp means to seize or take control of something by force, to dominate, or to arrogantly take something as if it is your right to it. In regard to a husband, a wife is never ever to take by force the authority to be the head of the home that has been given to the husband by God. Her instruction to her husband, therefore, is done in the spirit of humility, as one who understands her helpmate's role.

God said that *"It is not good for the man to be alone. I will make a helper who is just right for him"* **(Gen. 2:18 NLT)**. If a husband could do things on his own without his wife's help, then, why did God say that it was not good for him to be without her? Just as the Church needs the Holy Spirit's help to accomplish what God has called the Church to do, so too does the husband need his wife's help to accomplish what God has called him to do.

A name used in regard to the Holy Spirit is Paraclete. Literally it means, One who comes along side of. That is what you are to your husband also. You come along side of him to help and instruct. There is value that God has placed within you wives that your husband would be foolish to do without. Yet, if done with the wrong attitude or behavior, it could seem as if you were trying to control him and usurp his authority. Kind instruction, done in a spirit of humility, will help make the "proverbial medicine" go down smoother.

I = Instructor

Look at the way words can come out of your mouth and think about that when you are trying to instruct your husband. Which way do you think falls under that "kind instruction" mode?

> **James 3:5-6 MSG** *A word out of your mouth may seem of no account, but it can accomplish nearly anything—or destroy it! It only takes a spark, remember, to set off a forest fire. A careless or wrongly placed word out of your mouth can do that. By our speech we can ruin the world, turn harmony to chaos, throw mud on a reputation, send the whole world up in smoke and go up in smoke with it, smoke right from the pit of hell.*

OR

> **James 3:17-18 LB** *But the wisdom that comes from heaven is first of all pure and full of quiet gentleness. Then it is peace-loving and courteous. It allows discussion and is willing to yield to others; it is full of mercy and good deeds. It is wholehearted and straightforward and sincere. And those who are peacemakers will plant seeds of peace and reap a harvest of goodness.*

As a wife excels at kindly instructing her husband and as she becomes comfortable in her helpmates' role, God can then use her in the fullness of what He has defined as her role in this marital union. But just like husbands, wives need to keep the proper order of their assignments. As a wife, you must stay in the Word to insure the instruction you give to your husband is Godly instruction delivered in a spirit of kindness. Instruction delivered outside of this kindness presentation will fall on deaf ears. Remember, men receive communication through the frequency of honor. You will need to use all this information, all these tools, to make your case.

> **2 Timothy 2:23-26 NLT** *Again I say, don't get involved in foolish, ignorant arguments that only start fights. A servant of the Lord must not quarrel but must be kind to everyone, be able to teach, and be patient with difficult people. Gently instruct those who oppose the truth. Perhaps God will change those people's hearts, and they will learn the truth. Then they will come to their senses and escape from the devil's trap. For they have been held captive by him to do whatever he wants.*

A wife can kindly instruct her husband God's way and see the results promised in God's word OR she can do things the world, the flesh, or the devil's way and get no results and her husband remains captive. Only one way gets the job done correctly, it's **God's** Way.

> **Proverbs 31:11-12 NLT** *Her husband can trust her, and she will greatly enrich his life. She brings him good, not harm, all the days of her life.*

God has placed in wives a special wisdom and an ability to inspire trust in them from their spouses. I believe that old wives tale that "BEHIND EVERY GOOD MAN IS A GOOD WOMAN/WIFE." I believe that this is the sentiment behind this next Scripture verse because it is surrounded before and after by statements of how the godly wife is going about her duties.

> **Proverbs 31:23 NIV** *Her husband is respected at the city gate, where he takes his seat among the elders of the land.*

I = Instructor

While it is Christ who makes a man complete, it is the wife, through the Holy Spirit, who makes a husband whole. Remember where this all started; **Genesis 2:22 NKJV,** *Then the rib which the LORD God had taken from man He made into a woman, and He brought her to the man.* You can say then, that man needs his rib back – in the form of a woman – to be whole again. This is a perfect picture of what Christ was talking about when He said in **John 17:21 NKJV,** *"That they may all be one; as You Father are in Me and I in You, that they may be one in Us, that the world may believe that You have sent Me."*

There it is again… ONEness, it preaches the Gospel. God's desire to become one with us has no greater witness than in a marriage. As a husband and wife become one, they paint the picture for the entire world to see of the relationship God desires to have with us!

As women learn to Kindly Instruct their husbands, we will see changes in marriages. Men need help but it is help the way God planned on getting it to them. He has a way that will work, He has a plan that promises results and He has a promise that insures His presence. If wives will just learn to trust God by doing what He asks, we won't have any more Eves running around giving in to their desires, but we will become a body full of Marys whose hearts cry was, *"be it unto me according to your Word Lord!"*

TIME TO TALK

Does your husband resent it when you try to instruct him about something? Looking back, do you believe you have instructed him in the spirit of kindness? Has this instruction been wrapped in humility or was it delivered in a non-honorable way? Check yourself out, maybe even ask him.

Perhaps there are other reasons for him not receiving your instruction.

To those wives where the husband is not yet saved or perhaps is saved and is struggling with obedience, do you see the formula for creating an environment for God to send him repentance? Name the name commands God gives to His servants in order to create this environment. They are found in **2 Timothy 2:23-26 NLT.**

Chapter 16

W. I. *F*. E.

According to Proverbs 31 NLT we can see how a wife is to be a **W**orker to her family. She does this by ***I**nstructing* those in her care in the spirit of both wisdom and kindness. By becoming a ***F**riend*, she continues the process of ONEness with her husband. Through this godly, energetic lifestyle she becomes an ***E**xample* for her entire family, neighborhood, and community to follow.

F = *F*riend

Marriage causes us to live intimately with our spouses. With this great closeness demanded by marriage, it is paramount that husbands and wives live this life out not only as lovers and partners but as friends also. A husband needs the friendship of his wife to help him be successful. He will be a better performer in all areas of his life if his wife will undertake the mission of befriending her husband.

A wife's friendship with her husband is defined in great measure by her willingness to acknowledge his calling. She not only allows him to walk in it but she embraces the leadership role he exhibits by showing him a spirit of trust and cooperation.

> **Proverbs 31:11-12 AMP** *The heart of her husband trusts in her confidently and relies on and believes in her securely, so that he has no lack of honest gain or need of dishonest spoil. She comforts, encourages,*

and does him only good as long as there is life within her.

This is the perfect picture of friendship. The wife has proven so trustworthy (an earmark of friendship) that her husband has confidence in her and actually relies on and believes in her securely. **The New King James version** says *"The heart of her husband safely trusts her."*

Looking at the above Scripture, his trust for his wife is so strong that it produces something. This secure friendship between a man and his wife removes any temptation for him to cheat or rob or take something from someone else that does not belong to him. He can be honest and true in all his business dealings just because of this great friendship with his wife. Isn't it interesting how God's Word ties those two items together to create a biblical truth?

My secure, trusting friendship with my wife takes off the table any desire or temptation for me to profit though dishonest or ungodly gain. Wow!!!! That's awesome. I can assure you that I speak from experience on this one. We have a roofing company and there were many temptations offered to cheat a little here and there, misrepresent a quote on a job, just to secure that sale. Especially in hard times, when work was slow, it seemed to me that those temptations came a little more frequently. BUT God and my wife always kept me on the straight and narrow path. She would remind me of the Christian stand we had made for our Company. Even in really hard financial times, when we were so in need, never once did she ever cause me to cheat even a little bit. She never pressured me to do anything that we would later regret.

In times like that we became a **TEAM** – ***T**ogether **E**very **A**ttack **M**et.*

Instead, she would encourage me to look for ways to sow seed in times of famine. During those difficult or slow periods of time, I would not charge someone for a minor repair, as a way of sowing seed. My wife would support me in that decision rather than condemn me for not bringing home money that we so desperately needed. As that Scripture says, *"she comforts, encourages, and does him only good as long as there is life within her."* That fits my wife, perfectly.

That was not the case for Ananias and his wife Sapphira. Rather than telling him, "Thus saith the Lord, or Had not God said," she helped him to lie and cheat. The book of Proverbs says a lot about deceptive practices in business and the handling of money, but in this story, the consequences of that deception where DEADLY.

Acts 5:1-5 LB *But there as a man named Ananias (with his wife Sapphira) who sold some property, and brought only part of the money, claiming it was the full price. (His wife had agreed to this deception). The* **NIV** *says he did this "with his wife's full knowledge." But Peter said, "Ananias, Satan has filled your heart. When you claimed this was the full price, you were lying to the Holy Spirit. The property was yours to sell or not, as you wished. And after selling it, it was yours to decide how much to give. How could you do a thing like this? You weren't lying to us, but to God." As soon as Ananias heard these words, he fell to the floor, DEAD!*

Sapphira did not do her husband *"good as long as there was life within her,"* like she was suppose to and for her part in this deception, she too died.

My wife would always lay down her own wants and needs in order to support me and my decisions as head of home.

She loves me and willingly makes that sacrifice for me. My wife is my friend, my BEST FRIEND, and represents the greater love that Jesus talked about.

> **John 15:13 NKJV** *Greater love has no one than this, than to lay down one's life for his friends.*

After what Jesus has done for us, there is no greater example of someone laying down their life for a friend than the example of a wife entering into marriage. She gives up the absolute authority that life offers her when she willingly chooses to come along side her husband with the express desire to help him become the man that God has called him to be. With respect and honor and service to him, it enables him to fulfill his God given destiny.

The Godly wife does this all day, every day. In order to fully understand this, reread **Proverbs 31** and see how the ultimate reason for everything the wife is doing, is to win praise for her husband and to ensure his success. We use the term "friendship" loosely in our society, but when a wife truly embraces the biblical call to friendship within the marriage with her husband, we can see clearly God's intent regarding the virtue of friendship.

> **Proverbs 17:17 NKJV** *A friend loves at all times,* **The Message version** takes it a little deeper. *Friends love through all kinds of weather, and families stick together in all kinds of trouble.*

> **Proverbs 18:24 NKJV** *A man who has friends must himself be friendly, but there is a friend who sticks closer than a brother.*

My wife and I have had a running difference of opinion, not a disagreement which is dangerous to a relationship, but we look at something differently. Maybe it has to do with our background, our family history, and friendships in the past. My opinion is that I would rather be a child in a family. My wife's opinion is that she would rather be a friend of the family. Her reason is that, as part of a family, you are stuck with those people, but in a friendship, you are chosen to be there.

She would remind me of the *"friend who sticks closer than a brother."* How the Bible calls *"Abraham a friend of God"* and *"Abraham, Your friend forever."* That, *"the Lord would speak to Moses face to face, as one speaks to a friend."* Her reason is the **want to** factor rather than the **have to** factor. My response would be *"And if children, then heirs; heirs of God, and joint-heirs with Christ."* You get to go to the refrigerator any time you want and take out anything you want. A friend has to ask first.

I brought that up because my wife and I are not only family to one another, but we are **friends** also. We get the best of both worlds.

Proverbs 27:9 MSG *Just as lotions and fragrance give sensual delight, a sweet friendship refreshes the soul.*

The Amplified version – *oil and perfume rejoice the heart; so does the sweetness of a friend's counsel that comes from the heart.*

My wife's counsel means so very much to me. Her counsel is from her heart, it is sincere, and there is no deceit in it. I am so grateful for that aspect of my friendship with her.

Proverbs 27:17 NLT *As iron sharpens iron, so a friend sharpens a friend.*

My wife does sharpen me as iron sharpens iron. A sharpened tool is so much better to work with than a dull rusty tool. She helps make me better than I would be without her in my life. When a tool is being sharpened, pressure is applied and sparks are flying. I must admit it, there are times when my wife is sharpening me, the sparks are flying and my flesh wants to pull away. Through the years, I have come to trust my wife's friendship in this fact; she would never lie to me and that if she is that adamant about a thing, though my flesh rebels; stay with it and watch God do a work in me. Watch God make me a better instrument, a better tool, a better husband and father, a better teacher, a better minister, a better whatever HE needs me to be.

1 Peter 3:2 AMP *tells the wife to ...be devoted to, deeply love, and enjoy your husband.*

Enjoy... friends enjoy one another's company, they choose to spend time together, they don't have to, they want to. They share doing things together, they have common interests. They nurture and invest in their friendship; they deem it valuable to themselves. Look at what Jesus said concerning His want to:

John 17:24 NLT *Father, I want these [us] whom you have given me to be with me where I am.*

God's will for you wives is to *"enjoy your husband."* You can't enjoy him if you are always mad at him. Enjoying your husband is easy when husbands are doing well or they have brought their "A" game to the marriage. But what about when they are falling down, when they are under attack or under stress? When the last thing that you want to do is be around your husband let alone enjoy him. Let's go to the Word and see how God treated us and then see if it's practical to treat our husbands in the same manner.

Romans 5:8 NLT *But God showed HIS great love for us by sending Christ to die for us while we were still sinners.*

So we see here that *"God showed His great love to us ... while we were yet sinners."* Other translations say that He *"demonstrated His great love to us."* In other words, God did not just talk the talk, but he walked the walk. He put action to His love toward us, even when we did not deserve it. Are you wives capable of demonstrating your great love for your husband while he may yet be a sinner?

As Christians, despite our best efforts we will still stumble on occasion. I am not talking about being committed to sin; I am talking about not being perfect. Do you think that that was a surprise to God after He saved us? Do you think that God says "Boy, I screwed up; I never should have saved them and entered into covenant with them? Look at how they're behaving. How do I get out of this relationship with them?" Do you think God had "rose-colored glasses" on when he chose us?

Truth be told, God never has rose colored glasses on, He IS a rose colored glass. He always sees us as people who He greatly loves and always delights in. It's who He is and it is a promise He has made a vow that He will not break. That vow was to love us and to never leave us. PSSSSST... It's the same vow we made to each other when we got married.

Ephesians 2:4-5 AMP *But God, so rich is He in His mercy! because of and in order to satisfy the great and wonderful and intense love with which He loved us, Even when we were dead (slain) by our own shortcomings and trespasses, He made us alive together in fellowship and in union with Christ.*

His rich mercy is based on HIS INTENSE LOVE for us and not the other way around. So too should your mercy be for your husband. Your intense love for your husband is why you show him mercy, grace and forgiveness. Your intense love for your husband is why you should always enjoy your husband.

God expects the wife to enjoy her husband. It is part of the reverencing and the respecting part of our role as a wife to our husband. Ladies, step back and take pleasure in the man you married, remember "why" you married him, put aside his weaknesses and failures and practice enjoying just being around him again. Nurture the friendship part of your relationship that you once had with him; the laughter and the joy needs to return once again.

Even David, when he had been in the "dog house" with God because of his sin with Bathsheba, prayed, *"Do not banish me from your presence, and don't take your Holy Spirit from me. Restore to me the joy of your salvation,"* **(Ps. 51:11-12 NLT).** God had every reason to keep His distance from David, but He didn't.

Ladies, you may have every reason to keep your distance from your husband, but don't. God is a God of reconciliation and restoration of fellowship. My wife, Diane, would keep herself in the dog house and apart from me, when she was mad at me. It would go on for days and days. Now when she is angry or annoyed at me, she peeks into that "dog house" and decides she doesn't really want to go in there, it is much more fun being out **here playing with Ron.**

So Ladies, don't ever forget, he is still the man you married, the man you chose to love, he just needs your help and your friendship to remind him of that every day.

Song of Solomon 5:16 KJV

This is my beloved, and this is my friend.

TIME TO TALK

Friendship as the world views it and friendship as God views it are two totally different aspects of a relationship. What aspect of your friendship with your husband would confirm that statement?

Would you say that your friendship with your husband has grown to where he would say that "his heart safely trusts in you"? How so? If not, what could you do to help him feel that trust? Remember, this is about you creating trust… not him.

Would your husband say today that you are his best friend? Would you be willing to do whatever it takes to be that friend to him? Starting today, identify areas where you think you could improve. Talk to other women and see how they feel, then come up with a plan that would solidify that friendship. It may take a while, but the reward is great!

Chapter 17

W. I. F. *E.*

According to Proverbs 31 NLT we can see how a wife is to be a **W**orker to her family. She does this by **I**nstructing those in her care in the spirit of both wisdom and kindness. By becoming a **F**riend, she continues the process of ONEness with her husband. Through this godly, energetic lifestyle she becomes an **E**xample for her entire family, neighborhood, and community to follow.

E = *E*xample

God has placed the wife in marriage with the specific assignment to be an example to her husband and her children, her neighbors and her friends.

> **Proverbs 31:28-29 NLT** *Her children stand and bless her. Her husband praises her "There are many virtuous and capable women in the world, but you surpass them all!"*

Here, the wife's example of virtue and capability is noticed and complimented by her husband and her children. She excels so much at working, succeeding and at living a virtuous life that it is evident not only for her family to see, but so much so that they even talk about it. They especially think it is worth mentioning to her.

In **Titus 2:5 MSG** we see how older wives are to be examples to younger wives, showing them how to love their husbands. *By looking at them, the younger women will know* *how to love their husbands and children, be virtuous and pure, keep a good house, and be good wives.*

If we list the areas where the wives are to be an example and if we also list the people to whom she is to be an example to, we can create a clear picture of the sphere of influence in which these wives are being used by God in their marital ministry.

Wives are an example to: Their husband, their children, younger wives, and the public.

Wives are to be an example of: Purity, holiness, submission, and wisdom.

The example wives set for all to see goes so much further than those examples we have discussed. The anointing upon their lives to win their families through their example of holy, Godly living is so powerful. God promises salvation for their husbands if they will just do it. He promises their children will be saved, if they will just train them up through their example.

In **Hebrews**, God reveals how women of faith received their dead brought back to life. In **Colossians,** she is an example of obedience as she finds God's plan for her life through obedience to her husband. In **Romans**, she is the ultimate example of sacrifice as she risks her life for the cause of Christ. In **Acts**, she shows all how to fit in with the plans of her husband as Pricilla joins a ministry team with her husband. In **Ephesians**, she exemplifies honor as she teaches us honor through submission.

The list is long and her accomplishments are truly great as the Godly wife lives out Christ likeness again and again throughout Scripture. In **Titus**, she paints the picture of service by being her husband's helpmate at home. In **1 Corinthians**, she exemplifies the power of agreement as she gives her all for her husband. In **2 John** she exemplifies motherhood at its best as she receives praise for raising her children in truth.

Proverbs 31:20 NLT *She extends a helping hand to the poor and opens her arms to the needy.* Here the wife is an example of a giver.

Proverbs 31:25 NLT *She is clothed with strength and dignity, and she laughs without fear of the future.* Here the wife is an example of freedom from fear.

Proverbs 31:30 NLT *Charm is deceptive, and beauty does not last; but a woman who fears the LORD will be greatly praised.* Here the wife is an example of knowing where real beauty comes from.

1 Peter 3: 3-4 NLT *Don't be concerned about the outward beauty of fancy hairstyles, expensive jewelry, or beautiful clothes. You should clothe yourselves instead with the beauty that comes from within, the unfading beauty of a gentle and quiet spirit, which is so precious to God.* Again, the wife is an example of knowing where true beauty comes from.

1 Peter 3:5 NLT *This is how the holy women of old made themselves beautiful.*

They trusted God and accepted the authority of their husbands. Here, the wife is an example of trusting God and being submissive to their husbands.

Titus 2:3 NLT *Similarly, teach the older women to live in a way that honors God. They must not slander others or be heavy drinkers. Instead, they should teach others what is good.* Here, the wife is an example of honoring God in all she does. She sets the example of not being a gossip or an alcoholic, and others can follow the example she sets.

1 Timothy 3:11 *NLT* *In the same way, their [deacons] wives must be respected and must not slander others. They must exercise self-control and be faithful in everything they do.* Here again is a running theme of behavior for the wife to be an example.

Don't ever think that people are not watching your behavior, whether you are a good example or a bad one. Here, in **1 Timothy 5**, Paul is writing to Timothy talking about the virtuous behavior of widows.

1 Timothy 5:5 NLT *Now a true widow, a woman who is truly alone in this world, has placed her hope in God. She prays night and day, asking God for his help.*

1 Timothy 5:9-10 NLT *A widow who is put on the list for support must be a woman who is at least sixty years old and was faithful to her husband. She must be well respected by everyone because of the good she has done. Has she brought up her children well? Has she been kind to strangers and served other believers humbly? Has she helped those who are in trouble? Has she always been ready to do good?*

Ladies, you are truly great and you are truly anointed to bring the promises of God to pass, both in your own personal life and in the lives of those you love, by your example. Don't quit, don't ever give up. Sure, there will be times of frustration and disappointment. But God! He is able. Know that life, especially married life is not a sprint; it is a life long series of challenges lived out intimately with the man you have been called to help. Overcome the challenges through Christ and enjoy the victories, for our God loves you very much.

1 Corinthians 15:58 NKJV *Be steadfast, unmovable, always abounding in the work of the Lord, for you know that your labor in the Lord is not in vain.*

TIME TO TALK

Take stock of those around you, your husband, your friends, and your children. They are watching you. Are they praising you? Are they aware of the example you set in service to your spouse, so much so that they talk about it? In what ways can you set a better example? In what areas?

There were Bible references of wives who did certain things as they came alongside their husbands in Faith. If God were to include your name in the Bible in a new chapter today, what would He say about your service of faith to Him through your husband?

Chapter 18

Be the Woman/Wife God Has Called You To Be

If you want your husband to be the Man of God that you want him to be, you must be the Women of God that he needs you to be.

Ephesians 5:22-24 NLT *For wives, this means submit to your husbands as to the Lord. For a husband is the head of his wife as Christ is the head of the church. He is the Savior of his body, the church. As the church submits to Christ, so you wives should submit to your husbands in everything.*

In everything! Not some things, not just what I agree with, but the word of God says wives *are to be subject to their husbands in everything*. Those are not my words. They **are** the words of the Living God to wives. Therefore you need *to hearken to what the Spirit of God is saying* to you as a wife and be a *doer of the word instead of a hearer only* **(James 1:22 KJV).**

The word submit does not mean to be a slave to him, to always do what he tells you to do without question. Nor does it mean that you have no voice or say so in the matter. Remember, the Bible says *that it is not good for man to be alone, he needs a helpmate.* If man could make all the decisions by himself, then why would God say that he needs a wife to help him?

That word submit is the Greek word – hupatasso – and it means to willingly put yourself under the care and protection of someone else. In a marriage ceremony, doesn't the father of the bride relinquish his care and protection of his daughter when he is asked "Who gives this bride to this man?" This part of the ceremony is not just something we give the father of the bride to do because he is paying for the wedding.

When the minister asks, "Will you love and honor ... for better or worse, for richer and poorer, in sickness and in health etc." and you answer "I Will," then you have placed your life in the hands of your spouse for your care and protection.

Best case scenario is that your husband is doing all that it says to do in **Ephesians 5:22-33,** *Loving you as Christ loves the church, and sanctifying you and washing you with the water of the word.* That he *knows the voice of the Good Shepherd and does not follow the voice of the stranger* as it says in **John 10:3-5.** Then your job as a wife is easy. All is in perfect order and running smoothly.

Worst case scenario is that your husband is not following the Lord; not letting the *Holy Spirit lead him and guide him into all truth* **(John 16:13 KJV)**. Nor is he asking for God's help or yours in all the decision making processes. He may not even be saved at this point.

The word of God for you wife is still the same. It doesn't change based on your circumstances. For better or worse, it doesn't change. Wives are to *submit to your husbands as to the Lord.*

If he is not obeying the Lord in how he is acting, and then, wives don't obey the word of God in how they are acting, that leaves God only one course of action. He remains out of the picture totally. He can't step in and work on the situation if no one is being obedient to His Word and His Will for that marriage. God doesn't have the right to move in and make the necessary adjustments and force us to do things His way.

1 Peter 3:5-6 *NLT* *This is how the holy women of old made themselves beautiful. They trusted God and accepted the authority of their husbands. For instance, Sarah obeyed her husband, Abraham, and called him her master. You are her daughters when you do what is right without fear of what your husbands might do.*

The **Amplified version** says to *not give way to hysterical fears or letting anxieties unnerve you.* Let me ask you wives a question. Have you ever convinced your husband to change his mind by ranting or raving, or screaming and yelling, or just not speaking to him at all? How about *trusting God* instead when *accepting the authority of your husband?*

SARAH

Let's look at one of the most interesting characters in the Bible, Abraham's wife Sarah. There are many accounts of Sarah in the Bible. Her eagerness for a child, her doubt at God's promise for that child, her dominating Abraham with the fear of not having a child; but I wish to talk about Sarah in her role as the obedient wife.

Since the word of God uses Sarah as an example to us wives as to how we should fit in with the plans of our husband, even if they are not obeying God, let's look at how she handled a certain situation when Abraham was in fear rather than in faith.

Genesis 12:10-20 NLT *At that time a severe famine struck the land of Canaan, forcing Abram to go down to Egypt, where he lived as a foreigner. As he was approaching the border of Egypt, Abram said to his wife, Sarai, "Look, you are a very beautiful woman. When the Egyptians see you, they will say, 'This is his wife. Let's kill him; then we can have her!' So please tell them you are my sister. Then they will spare my life and treat me well because of their interest in you."*

And sure enough, when Abram arrived in Egypt, everyone spoke of Sarai's beauty. When the palace officials saw her, they sang her praises to Pharaoh, their king, and Sarai was taken into his palace. Then Pharaoh gave Abram many gifts because of her—sheep, goats, cattle, male and female donkeys, male and female servants, and camels.

*But the L*ORD *sent terrible plagues upon Pharaoh and his household because of Sarai, Abram's wife. So Pharaoh summoned Abram and accused him sharply. "What have you done to me?" he demanded. "Why didn't you tell me she was your wife? Why did you say, 'She is my sister,' and allow me to take her as my wife? Now then, here is your wife. Take her and get out of here!" Pharaoh ordered some of his men to escort them, and he sent Abram out of the country, along with his wife and all his possessions.*

Abraham faltered in his trust in God when he told Sarah to say she was his sister only. By failing to tell the whole truth, namely that she was also his wife; he was walking by sight and his own knowledge and understanding of the situation, instead of by faith. Do you think she was willing to be part of this king's harem? Whether she agreed with him or not, she submitted to his authority and plan, and that is why God had a place in which He could intervene on their behalf.

Even if you don't think your husband is right, by obeying the word of God for YOUR life, you give God a place in which to work. God was able to redeem that situation and spare their lives all because of Sarah's willingness to submit to Abraham's leadership.

Genesis 20:1–17 NLT gives us another account of Abraham doing the exact same thing a second time. And again, I believe that all was spared because of Sarah's ability to submit to her husband whether she agreed with him or not. Do you think she would have at least reminded him about what had happened the last time he pulled a stunt like this? Or how close she had come to being in a king's harem? Or just because they got away with it the last time doesn't mean they can get away with it again the second time.

Yet she did again submit to her husband's authority, and again God had room in which to maneuver, and again they were delivered out of that situation.

Now remember, Sarah was not always correct in the things she made Abraham do either. In **Genesis 16** she pushed him to go into her maid when she was desperate to have a child. To this day the entire Middle East and the world suffer because of the hostilities between the Arabs and the Jews. Eve though, is the best of the worst examples of a wife influencing her husband to do something wrong. Man is still under the penalty of sin for what she convinced her husband to do.

God doesn't hold Eve or Sarah responsible for those things, but He does hold the man of God as head responsible. The "Buck Stops With Them" you can say. So don't be so quick to blame your husband if he doesn't instantly submit to your will concerning a matter. Your way may not be correct in the handling of the matter either.

Well, how does a godly woman act when confronted by a decision she thinks is wrong. She adheres to the word of God in every area, at all times.

> **2 Timothy 2:23-26 NLT** *Again I say, don't get involved in foolish, ignorant arguments that only start fights. A servant of the Lord must not quarrel but must be kind to everyone, be able to teach, and be patient with difficult people. Gently instruct those who oppose the truth. Perhaps God will change those people's hearts, and they will learn the truth. Then they will come to their senses and escape from the devil's trap. For they have been held captive by him to do whatever he wants.*

Ranting and raving and giving your husband a piece of your mind never ever gets the job done. Trusting God and doing things God's way works all the time.

> **Hebrews 10:35–39 NLT** *So do not throw away this confident trust in the Lord. Remember the great reward it brings you! Patient endurance is what you need now, so that you will continue to do God's will. Then you will receive all that he has promised. "For in just a little while, the Coming One will come and not delay. And my righteous ones will live by faith. But I will take no pleasure in anyone who turns away." But we are not like those who turn away from God to their own destruction. We are the faithful ones, whose souls will be saved.*

If you care about seeing **God's will be done** in your family, *as it is done in heaven*, then again you have to do things God's way, without fear.

> **1 John 5:14-15 NKJV** *Now this is the confidence that we have in Him, that if we ask anything according to His will, He hears us. And if we know that He hears us, whatever we ask, we know that we have the petitions that we have asked of Him.*

ABIGAIL

Intercession can take on many forms. Wives can be intercessors for their husbands in the realm of the Spirit though an active prayer life. They can be intercessors for the husbands in the natural realm as they come between their husband and adversity. As we remember that God's calling on a wife is to her husband, we can see the importance that this particular role will play.

My wife speaks words of wisdom to me, and keeps me from making perhaps a bad business decision. She may come between me and an irate homeowner or customer. There are many ways that Godly wives fill this role, but my favorite in the Bible is when Abigail went to bat for her husband Nabal.

If you recall, Nabal was a fool. Actually, his name means fool. How such a man ever married such a great lady is beyond me, nevertheless, they were husband and wife.

> **1 Samuel 25:3 NKJV** *The name of the man was Nabal, and the name of his wife Abigail. And she was a woman of good understanding and beautiful appearance; but the man was harsh and evil in his doings. He was of the house of Caleb.*

David's herdsman protected Nabal's sheep and his shepherds from attack by bandits throughout the year. David, at the end of that year came to receive a gift from Nabal for those services. Nabal reacted poorly and was not going to give him anything. David got angry and was going to destroy Nabal's entire holdings, his livestock, his home and his family. Abigail got wind of this and acted quickly and wisely to keep this from happening.

> **1 Samuel 25:18 MSG** *Abigail flew into action. She took two hundred loaves of bread, two skins of wine, five sheep dressed out and ready for cooking, a bushel of roasted grain, a hundred raisin cakes, and two hundred fig cakes, and she had it all loaded on some donkeys. Then she said to her young servants, "Go ahead and pave the way for me. I'm right behind you." But she said nothing to her husband Nabal.*

By her quick action, she averted the destruction of her household. Look at what she says as she approaches David.

> **1 Samuel 25:23 MSG** *As soon as Abigail saw David, she got off her donkey and fell on her knees at his feet, her face to the ground in homage, saying, "My master, let me take the blame! Let me speak to you. Listen to what I have to say.*

Check this out, Abigail not only interceded for Nabal by coming between him and David's wrath, but she took the blame and was willing to take the punishment as well. This example of intercession should cause wives to look at the way they deal with their husband's failings in a new light. She put her life on the line in order to preserve her husband and her family... and she succeeded.

You might think that this was an extreme example and a life and death situation of this sort could never happen in you home. I have news for you, it happens every day. Husbands are under supernatural attack every day. We turn on the television and we are tempted sexually. We go to the office and the temptation to cut corners or compromise to make that big sale is right out there. Tax time comes and the temptation arises to make deductions we should not make.

We husbands need our wives, coming between us and sin in the realm of the Spirit. We need our wives praying for us to be able to stand against these attacks. *"It is not good for man to be alone."* We must have help.

> **Ecclesiastes 4:9-12 NLT** *Two people are better off than one, for they can help each other succeed. If one person falls, the other can reach out and help. But someone who falls alone is in real trouble. Likewise, two people lying close together can keep each other warm. But how can one be warm alone? A person standing alone can be attacked and defeated, but two can stand back-to-back and conquer.*

Wives, be aware of your role as your husband's intercessor. He needs one here on this earth. He has Jesus in heaven, but God sent you into his life to fulfill that role here. No one else is going to do it for him, no one else can do it as good as you can. Remember, you are **ONE** flesh. It is yours to do with as you will. Don't fail them!

Be the Woman/Wife that God has called you to be and watch your husband become the Man/Husband that God has called him to be also.

TIME TO TALK

Can you think of an area in your relationship with your husband today where you are currently wearing the mantel of intercessor?

Often, the wife's chief role as intercessor takes on a spiritual tone. The husband is not saved, or he's not submitting to God. Isn't it wonderful that God knows exactly what we husbands need? What do you do to stay strong during these times when it looks like God is not moving?

Have you discovered your husband's needs through this intercession? Husbands don't like to reveal their weaknesses to their wives. Often times the things that we see bothering them are just symptoms and not the real issue. Can you recall a time where God supernaturally revealed to you what your husband really needed in the midst of your intercession?

Chapter 19

Protecting your Husband
(When sin rears its ugly head)

Let's say you find out that your husband has been sinning, perhaps caught dabbling in pornography. He may have tried to get free from that and stop doing it, but he soon realizes that he's trapped. He's being held captive by that sin and it's now become a stronghold in his life.

STRONGHOLD means something has a strong physical, emotional and spiritual hold on a person. A strong grip on someone's life and it won't let go. As a wife, you have a choice as to what to do.

OPTION #1

You can start yelling and screaming at him, putting him down, and making him feel ashamed. You can start speaking out all your fears and worries and without realizing it, you are giving power to those fears with your words. The result of that is that he shifts his focus from trying to fight the enemy, which is the world, the flesh and the devil, and starts fighting you instead. When he starts fighting back at you, you get all offended and feel mistreated which makes you feel justified in mistreating him that much more. Round and round you both go, but in the mean time the devil is standing there laughing. He has you BOTH exactly where he wants you. Your husband is trapped in pornography and you are trapped in unforgiveness with perhaps a root of bitterness starting to take hold.

The Bible says in **Ephesians 6:12 NLT** *For we are not fighting against flesh-and-blood enemies,* [your husband or your wife] *but against evil rulers and authorities of the unseen world, against mighty powers in this dark world, and against evil spirits in the heavenly places.* But by doing the above option #1, you are fighting with flesh and blood and therefore you both are ignoring the real enemy. Plus, what did Jesus say in **Luke 11:17 NIV,** *"Any kingdom divided against itself will be ruined, and a house divided against itself will fall."* **The New Living Translation** says, *"A family splintered by feuding will fall apart."*

Also, concerning the above option, the wife putting down her husband, trying to make him feel ashamed; who has she aligned herself with? **Revelation 12:10 NKJV** says that the devil is *the accuser of the brethren, who accused them before our God night and day.* That is not part of the wife's job description. Even in prayer, realizing the danger her husband is in, her attitude should be one of rescuing him rather than accusing him.

Therefore, what is the wife's role when she sees that her husband is being held captive by the devil, and that he's trapped in the stronghold of sin?

OPTION #2

Revelation 12:11 NKJV says *that they overcame him [the devil, the accuser] by the blood of the Lamb and by the word of their testimony.* Jesus already provided the *blood of the Lamb,* now it's up to you to provide the *word of your testimony.* What word is that? That you forgive your husband and remind him that God will forgive him also; that you are there to help him break free from this stronghold. Then you start speaking into him what the word of God says about him.

That he is more than a conqueror. **Romans 8:37 KJV**

That he can do all things through Christ who strengthens him. **Philippians 4:13 NKJV**

That the joy of the Lord is his strength. **Nehemiah 8:10 KJV**

That greater is He that is within him then he that is in the world. **1 John 4:4 KJV**

He is walking in the Spirit and not fulfilling the lust of the flesh. **Galatians 5:16 KJV**

He walks worthy of the Lord in all pleasing. **Colossians 1:10 KJV**

He is the Head and not the tail. **Deuteronomy 28:13 KJV**

Picture it this way. In the old *Popeye the Sailor Man* cartoons, when Popeye was getting beat up by Bluto, what was his lady Olive Oyl trying to do? She was trying to get the spinach to Popeye. She knew that if she could get that spinach into him, he'd get the strength he needed to kick Bluto's butt.

Well ladies, when you are speaking God's word by faith over your husband in his time of need, you are providing him with the spiritual strength that he needs to break free *from the sin that so easily besets him* **(Heb. 12:1 KJV).** That so called, spiritual spinach, doesn't do a bit of good while it sits on a shelf in a can. The power comes when the word is spoken and received.

When you *call those things that be not as though they were* **(Rom. 4:17 KJV)**, you are literally changing *those things that we see which are temporal and subject to change* **(2 Cor. 4:18 KJV),** to those things that are eternal and will last forever. When you give your husband God's truth instead of the devils lies, the bible says that *knowing the truth WILL set him free* **(John 8:32 KJV).**

It's important to remember **2 Corinthians 10:3-5 KJV,** *For though we walk in the flesh, we do not war according to the flesh. For the weapons of our warfare are not carnal but mighty in God for pulling down strongholds. Casting down imaginations, and every high thing that exalteth itself against the knowledge of God, and bringing into captivity every thought to the obedience of Christ;*

What if your husband does not want to eat that "spiritual spinach"? Then as my wife Diane would say, I'm going to do what it says to do in **Ephesians 6:10-11 KJV.** I'm going to *be strong in the Lord and the power of His might.* I'm going to *put on the whole armor of God that I may be able to stand against the wiles of the devil.* I'm not going to wrestle with my husband *but against principalities, against powers, against the rulers of the darkness of this world, against spiritual wickedness in high places.*

This is my husband I'm going to battle for, my marriage and my family. You think that I am going to let the devil steal, kill and destroy **(John 10:10 KJV)** what means the most to me. NO WAY!!!!!!!!

I'm going to do what God does in **Psalm 32:7 KJV** and sing ***songs of deliverance*** over him. I'm going to

2 Corinthians 2:14 KJV and *thank God who always causes us to triumph in Christ Jesus.*

In other words, I'll eat that "spiritual spinach" myself and do battle with "Bluto" myself because *if God be for me who can be against me and with God all things are possible* **(Matt. 19:26 KJV)**. If small boyish David can take down giant Goliath because of his covenant with God, then this "little woman" can take down any giants that would come against me, my husband or my family because of the covenant I have with God. That's how Diane would handle that.

Now ladies, just one more thing. You can serve that "spiritual spinach" to your husband every day and help keep him full of spiritual strength, which in turn can keep him from falling into traps that the devil sets up for him, or you can keep it in the pantry and wait until trouble comes and then try to feed it to your husband. Your choice!!!!

Getting God's Power on the Scene

There are many ways to get God's power on the scene on behalf of your husband. Let's look at another way of getting your husband what he needs during his time of trial or testing or out and out sinning.

2 Timothy 2:24-26 KJV *And the servant of the Lord [that's you wife] must not strive; but be gentle unto all men, apt to teach, patient, in meekness instructing those that oppose themselves; if God peradventure will give them repentance to the acknowledging of the truth; And that they may recover themselves out of the snare of the devil, who are taken captive by him at his will.*

Look at the power here available to you ladies if you want it. God says in this Scripture that He will send repentance to your husband. But you must first create the environment for Him to be able to do that. Let's look at the environment you need to create.

#1 You must not strive with him. God cannot work in that kind of environment where there is fighting and quarreling and arguments going on.

#2 You must be gentle. No exploding going on. No hurling of bombs. No threats.

#3 You must be able to teach your husband. There is a way you can let your husband know that what he is doing is wrong and why, without disrespecting or dishonoring him. My wife uses this phrase, "A Point of Information." It requires no immediate response on my part. It does not put me in a corner where I need to defend myself either. It is just information that she thinks I need to know in order for ME to properly evaluate the situation.

#4 You must be patient. Once you have given the information to your husband, through the frequency of honor and respect, you give him time to digest it. To mull it over and hopefully pray about it. You are also giving God time to speak to his heart.

#5 You are doing this instructing with meekness, with a servant's heart in humility. That means you don't have the "Gotcha" attitude going on, or the "I knew you were going to do that" superiority attitude either.

You are allowed to correct your husband's errant behavior, but you are doing it in the presentation of the Holy

Spirit and not in your flesh. There is a world of difference. One, wounds, and dishonors your husband and renders God unable to work on your behalf. The other brings about your desires... God sending repentance to him. The next part is so important. If you do what you are supposed to do, then once again you have granted God permission for your husband to receive truth and escape from the enemy's grip.

Despite whether you agree with this statement or not, it is true nonetheless. The key to your husband's freedom is in your hands, not his. We did not have the power to save ourselves from the wages of sin. It took a Savior, a Redeemer, an Intercessor; it took Jesus. Jesus, who was willing to pay whatever price was necessary to see us set free. Will you do the same for your husband? Well, it is going to take you following the Holy Spirit to save your husband from the mess that he is in.

When God made you one flesh, He equipped you with everything you need for the long haul. He put things inside of you that your husband needs and He put things inside of your husband that you need. Draw on those things especially when trouble times arise.

When your flesh wants to rise up and pitch a fit, WILL YOU lay that flesh down sacrificially and put on a gentle and quiet spirit instead?

1 Peter 3:4 NLT *You should clothe yourselves instead with the beauty that comes from within, the unfading beauty of a gentle and quiet spirit, which is so precious to God.*

WILL YOU restore your husband back into fellowship with you? **Galatians 6:1 MSG** *If someone falls into sin, forgivingly restore him, saving your critical comments for yourself.*

WILL YOU give things the time necessary? **Ephesians 4:2 LB** *Be patient with each other, making allowance for each other's faults because of* ***your love***.

In **Hebrews 11 NLT** we read about the men and women of faith who endured many serious trials and tests and came out the other side victorious. **Verse 35** in particular says that, *Women received their loved ones back again from death.* If they can do that by faith then you surely can receive your loved one, your husband, back from *that sin that has so easily beset him* **(Heb. 12:1 KJV)**.

James 1:2-4 LB says, *"Dear brothers, is your life full of difficulties and temptations?"* Then be happy—does it really say to BE HAPPY when you are going through difficult situations? Yes it does!—*for when the way is rough, your patience has a chance to grow. So let it grow, and don't try to squirm out of your problems. For when your patience is finally in full bloom, then you will be ready for anything, strong in character, full and complete."*

When you allow God to use you to help your husband escape from the sin or the temptation that has got him trapped, not only will your husband be rewarded but you will receive a reward also. God does not waste anything that you may be going through.

SO – What are you going to do?

Hebrews 10:35–39 NLT *So do not throw away this confident trust in the Lord. Remember the great reward it brings you! Patient endurance is what you need now, so that you will continue to do God's will. Then you will receive all that he has promised. "For in just a little while, the Coming One will come and not* *delay. And my righteous ones will live by faith. But I will take no pleasure in anyone who turns away." But we are not like those who turn away from God to their own destruction. We are the faithful ones, whose souls will be saved.*

There is your starting point: Confident trust in the Lord, patient endurance, continue to do God's will, and then, RECEIVE.

NOW – What?

1 John 5:14–15 NKJV *Now this is the confidence that we have in Him, that if we ask anything according to His will, He hears us. And if we know that He hears us, whatever we ask, we know that we have the petitions that we have asked of Him.*

There is your ending point: Confidence in His will, we ask, we HAVE.

The choice is yours ladies. What kind of life do you wish to live with your husband? Even though we men may act like it at times, we don't need our wives to be our moms. We need you to be helpmates of the highest order. We need you to be full of the wisdom and power of God. We need you to be open to receiving instruction from the Holy Ghost and passing that instruction along to us in an honest, honorable and straightforward manner.

God has placed that need within men and it is filled by wives. That's a large part of the ONEness process. Of course your husband is going to mess up. Of course they need help, that's what you signed on for! Remember, we said for better or for worse at our marriage ceremony. Well, sometimes it is the worse, but in marriage quitting isn't allowed. It is not an option that is put on the table. I don't believe that's who you ladies are. I believe that those of you who read this book are God's finest!

Part Four

Chapter 20

HELP IS HERE

If you ever want to know what's important to God, just look at the things that are under attack. In America today, right at the top of the list is Marriage and Families. Never before has the fabric of marriage been ripped apart, been called into question or been turned upside down. Today's society has to debate what marriage is. This is in the face of the clear and present truths that have been presented in the Bible. Traditional values are under attack and our nation is on the verge of total moral chaos.

It doesn't have to be like this. Those of us who are Christians have the ability, NO, we have the responsibility to use our marriages as beacon lights for the floundering masses. God is not a God that wastes. He has created the world in which we live with opportunities for us to find Him just about everywhere.

In our opinion marriage is the easiest, most visible platform in which God can be seen. He pulls out all the stops in His efforts to use a husband to show his family what God Himself looks like. From allowing husbands to wear His name to the command to be a provider for our family, His love is manifested through us as we endeavor to make Him more real to those we love.

In His finest wisdom He offers husbands helpmates who can guide them towards the spiritual side of life. God knows what is happening at this late hour, He knows the full force of the attack against marriage and He has equipped them to stand. His plan doesn't have any failure to it. His Word is strong and victorious just like it has always been. The challenge that we face in order to be successful at marriage is how will we withstand this attack?

This book has not only pointed husbands and wives in the direction of that victory; it has placed victory in your very hands. God has placed His plan for marriage in His book. We have taken His plan for marriage, we have dug it out of His book and we have placed it right here. Truth be told, you could have dug this out for yourselves, but God has allowed us to do it for you.

The truth is, you don't even need this book, the Bible is sufficient for itself to fill your every spiritual need. But we have broken down the Scriptures and we have made them palatable to you so that perhaps the truth of God might be more easily digested. You too have the ability to open the Bible and find Paul writing to husbands, encouraging them to *"love their wives as Christ loves the Church."* You could have read on and seen where Paul paints the picture of how we are to do that, as he tells us to give *"our lives to our wives as Christ did it for the Church."* To wash our wives daily with *"the washing water of the Word."* You could have also discovered that Jesus is *"ever living to make intercession for the saints"* the picture of how husbands are to be ever living to make intercession for our wives.

All that and more is still there, all that wisdom and instruction is ever present for you to tap into. We have filled this book with Scripture because Scripture is ALIVE and POWERFUL! Our words are nice and they have value in encouragement and enlightenment, but we must have LIFE for our marriages. That's the only thing that will secure your marriage in today's social atmosphere.

place in their marriage, are now beacons of light to couples around them. They are sharing with others the things that they have learned and applied in their marriage.

You don't have to touch a generation. All you have to do is let God use your marriage to touch your children. Perhaps a family member, a neighbor or a co-worker will notice. Who knows, maybe you will begin to share these truths in a small Bible study. Your Godly marriage is not just for you, but it is for everyone you know. You are equipped, you are ready you are ordained by the Creator Himself to use your marriage for His purpose and glory.

For this reason shall (fill in your name)_____ leave his father and mother and be joined unto his wife and the two shall become one glad messenger of good tidings. Here's praying that your

Marriage is **ONE**derful too!

In days gone by we might have encouraged you to "fall in love with the Word." We know better now and falling in love with something means you are under control by your emotions and we know that that is not how Christians live. We will encourage you to "choose to love the Word."

Before we head out in the morning and enter into the realm of the ungodly we must be prepared for the temptations we will face. We must be armed, ready and able to keep at arms length the subtle attempts that will get us off our faith. We must have spent time with the Creator of all life. We must know the difference between good and evil, right and wrong. We must be able to discern between faith and fear, and truth or trick; and we must be able to turn our backs on compromise.

Most of us have heard the phrase "Generational Curse" or we are familiar with the Scripture about a father's sin being visited upon his family for four generations to come. These phrases are talking about building a legacy for our families. It's not too late. We can begin creating new legacies in our homes today.

We can start by creating the legacy that says divorce is not an option. We can build a legacy that will insure that our children's marriages will be built on solid ground. We can end for once and for all the divorce cycle in our families. It's marriage in its absolute truest sense. We have the opportunity to not only prevent divorce from happening in our homes, but we have the privilege of finally revealing for all to see, what marriage is supposed to look like.

We pray this book has upped your expectations. We hope this book has encouraged you and lifted your heart concerning your spouse. Truth is, we know it has. We hear it from couple after couple that have attended our classes. We have seen and heard how couples, who were in a very dark

Do you need a speaker?

Do you want Ron and Diane Geyer to speak to your group or event? Then contact Larry Davis at: (623) 337-8710 or email: ldavis@intermediapr.com or use the contact form at: www.intermediapr.com.

Whether you want to purchase bulk copies of *Marriage Needs Maintenance* or buy another book for a friend, get it now at: www.imprbooks.com.

If you have a book that you would like to publish, contact Terry Whalin, Publisher, at Intermedia Publishing Group, (623) 337-8710 or email: twhalin@intermediapub.com or use the contact form at: www.intermediapub.com.